Björn Vierhaus

Detail Drawing

Björn Vierhaus

Detail Drawing

BIRKHÄUSER
BASEL

Contents

Foreword

Details have a special importance in the design of buildings, since they reflect, in a small part, the complexity of the architecture. Details contain information about the joining of components, and how the requirements of construction and building physics are satisfied; they also contribute significantly to the quality of the building. In addition to conceptual and technical aspects, details convey information specific to the different building trades; they determine the qualities of surfaces in terms of appearance and touch. Last but not least, details clarify jointing principles and determine the sequence of the different tasks to be carried out, thereby impacting on the coordination of trades and the schedule of work.

Details are therefore an important element of architectural design, usually providing an illustrated guide to all important geometric contexts. Detail drawings are particularly suitable for communicating the various elements of information to the operatives in a kind of universal language.

For a drawing to be suitable as an accurate instruction for the performance of building work, it needs to contain all relevant information and be clear and concise. This detail drawing volume is not intended as a collection of examples of construction details, but as a teaching guide that acquaints the reader in a step-by-step process with the creation of detailed construction drawings.

Building on the reader's general knowledge of technical drawing, this volume sets out the specific requirements applicable to detail drawings.

By explaining all typical elements of a detail drawing, the reader is given a type of 'tool box', and – with the help of realistic construction examples – the path towards the independent creation of high-quality detail drawings is demonstrated.

Bert Bielefeld, Editor

Introduction

Generally speaking, a detail is an individual element or a part of a larger whole. The term *detail* derives from the verb *détailler* in the French language. It can be translated as 'separating' or 'taking apart to form individual parts.' This already explains an important characteristic of a detail: the detail is a part of other elements which has been detached from the whole. The word *detail* does not refer to the smallest object that cannot be further subdivided, for example a single screw, but to a defined collection of individual parts – for example, the fixing of a railing to a building. What is a detail?

A clear distinction can be made between a miniature and a detail; while a miniature represents the whole at a reduced scale, a detail represents a small part of the whole at a larger scale or even at true scale. Miniature

The perception of the details of buildings varies a great deal from person to person, and often takes place in processes that cannot be measured. For example, when one only takes a fleeting look at a building, the main detail perceived may just be the color scheme. Alternatively, the most conspicuous detail may be the materials used for the building. However, these elements do not initially play a major role in detail design. Instead, detail design focuses primarily on how individual building components fit together, for example, the joining details of construction. Perception of details

Compared to the working drawing at a scale of 1:50 in which the entire building is explained and illustrated with the help of additional drawings such as layout plans, sections, and elevations, the detail drawing only deals with a small part which is shown in greater detail. Working drawing

The basic method is very similar; the working drawing presents the different parts of the building in a set order (for example, exterior walls, interior walls, rooms with openings) and shows how these parts (including any other elements such as staircases) relate to one another in order to meet the overall design requirements.

The detail drawing, on the other hand, coordinates the individual elements of a functional relationship (such as a window frame, windowsill, external wall insulation), including other elements (for example, a fastening bracket and sealing compound), taking into account the design requirements and the technical rules of application.

Basics and Requirements

In order to explain the basics and requirements pertaining to the detail design process, we will illustrate the characteristics of detail design drawings in the following chapter and provide an overview of the purposes the drawings may be used for.

EXPLANATION OF TERMS, AND THEIR USE IN DETAIL DRAWINGS

Precise building instruction

The detail drawing is a precise building instruction for individual parts of a building. In this phase, the architect determines how exactly the individual parts fit together. For the architect therefore, the detail drawing is a logical continuation of the design process.

A meaningful detail drawing is an important information medium conveying the architect's design intention to the construction workers on the building site. Most of the time, the contents of these drawings are implemented without changes.

Source document for documentary evidence

Detail drawings are also used as source documents for various checks and calculations, which are normally carried out by other participants in the construction project. An important part of detail design is to place all construction particulars into a specific order. During this process it is quite common for issues to arise that must be clarified by specialist engineers participating in the design process. It is usual for the input information based on which the documentary evidence is prepared to be provided in the form of a draft version of the respective detail design.

For example, detail drawings are used to establish the structural design of screw fixings or to calculate whether thermal bridging occurs in certain construction elements.

Source document for specifications

Detail drawings are also used as a basis for describing the required construction work; they help to formulate the specification, and show the particular application in each case.

Source document for ordering materials

Construction companies use detail drawings provided with the tender documents to order the appropriate amount of materials and to purchase prefabricated products with the specified dimensions and properties.

Source document for accounting purposes

In addition to using plan and section drawings for the accounts of construction work, detail drawings are used for establishing exact quantities. Careful and thorough annotation and complete dimensional information on all important elements prevent misunderstandings and avoid disputes between the contract partners.

GENERAL REQUIREMENTS FOR A DETAIL DRAWING

Various general requirements have to be met to ensure that detail drawings can be used for the above purposes:

1. The geometric dimensions must be shown

The dimensions of all parts are shown in the detail drawings. Where building components are to be fabricated by construction workers, they refer to the detail drawings for the required dimensions to which they build the respective components. Where prefabricated parts are used, the information in the detail drawings is used for ordering the respective products. > Fig. 1

2. A check for collisions in all three dimensions must be made

Detail drawings are used to check whether there are any conflicts between the different building components. In order to avoid any geometric conflict or collision it is important to illustrate the situation from several angles.

Similar principles apply to detail drawings as to those applicable in scheme design and working drawings: in order to present an entire building, it is necessary to show layout plans, sections, and elevations. In order to show all relevant aspects of a detail as a small part of the whole, it is also necessary to show the detail from several angles. > Fig. 2

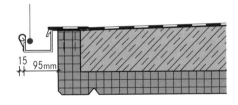

box gutter made of titanium zinc,
preweathered, NG 200
Installed with fall of 3 mm/m,
with support bracket

15   95mm

Fig. 1: Dimensions in the detail drawing

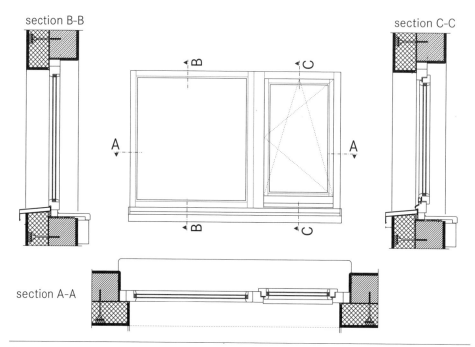

section B-B

section C-C

section A-A

Fig. 2: Presentation of a functional relationship in elevation, section, and plan

3. Suitability for purpose should be checked

Accurate detail drawings can be used to enter and check the dimensions required to ensure suitability for purpose. This often applies to the clear dimensions of door and window openings. In addition, the dimensions of escape routes are often critical for establishing suitability for
● purpose.

4. Buildability and accessibility must be checked

Detail drawings are used to check the technical feasibility of the planned building component and to provide evidence of this. This also includes a check as to whether the individual parts can be reached by the construction crew for the purpose of the installation, or whether they are
● obstructed by other components.

● **Example:** Is a 1.01 m-wide opening in the shell building wide enough to fit a window with a clear glazed dimension of 90 cm? This can be checked with the help of a detail drawing. > Fig. 3

● **Example:** For the purpose of inserting a screw, it is important to ensure that there is sufficient space for the tool needed to insert the screw. It is also important to take account of the sequence in which the building components are installed. > Fig. 4

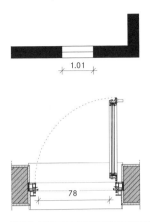

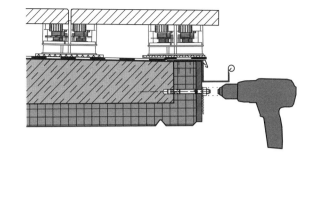

Fig. 3: Clear dimensions of openings in the shell building and in fitted components

Fig. 4: Accessibility to individual components

5. Communicating finer details of the design intention and ensuring that they are feasible

Depending on the design, it is possible that the appearance of an entire building is determined by the design of details. The design drawings are used to design, determine, and convey these details.

For example, the following figure shows a window fitted centrally to the depth of the exterior wall on the left and, on the right, a window fitted flush with the outside surface of the exterior wall. > Fig. 5

The installation of window elements flush with the exterior surface of the wall must be carefully detailed.

Installation details of windows and doors significantly influence the character of the building. The design of the eaves and verges of this building are also details that influence its overall geometric impression. > Fig. 6

6. Individual elements must be fitted together to ensure their proper function

The individual elements of a functional relationship are arranged in the detail drawing to ensure that they function properly and appear as intended. > Fig. 7

7. The installation sequence is determined

The detail drawing helps the construction crew to understand the sequence in which individual components are to be installed. As a rule, the completed situation is shown in the drawing. A step-by-step building instruction, such as one can find with furniture, is only used for very complex details or in situations where an uncommon building method is called for.

Fig. 5: Installation position of window elements

Fig. 6: Enhancing the appearance of a fairly ordinary domestic building through careful choice of details

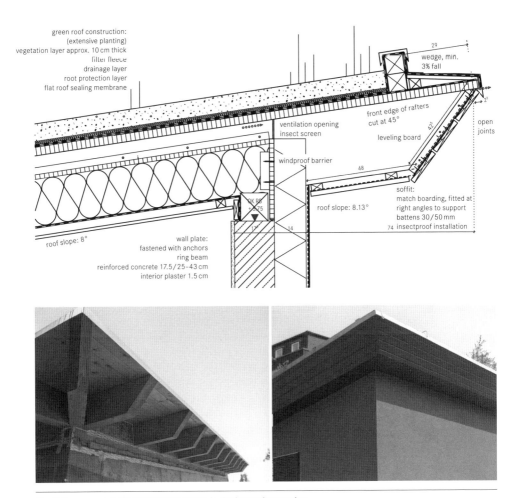

green roof construction:
(extensive planting)
vegetation layer approx. 10 cm thick
filter fleece
drainage layer
root protection layer
flat roof sealing membrane

29
wedge, min.
3% fall

front edge of rafters
cut at 45°

ventilation opening
insect screen

leveling board

open
joints

windproof barrier

48

roof slope: 8.13°

soffit:
match boarding, fitted at
right angles to support
battens 30/50 mm
74 insectproof installation

roof slope: 8°

wall plate:
fastened with anchors
ring beam
reinforced concrete 17.5/25–43 cm
interior plaster 1.5 cm

Fig. 7: Arrangement of individual elements in design and execution

8. The joining method should be indicated

The detail drawing shows the operatives what method is used to join the individual components. > Fig. 8

9. Material properties and treatments can be indicated

The designer may choose to indicate product characteristics or treatment methods in the detail drawing. As a rule, this is done by adding text to the drawn object. The product characteristics must be accurately specified in order to ensure that they satisfy the design intention. Example: 'Coated with several layers of plastic coating, RAL color shade 7016.'

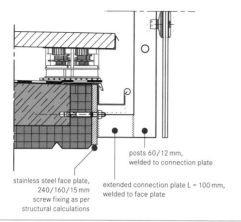

posts 60/12 mm,
welded to connection plate

stainless steel face plate,
240/160/15 mm
screw fixing as per
structural calculations

extended connection plate L = 100 mm,
welded to face plate

Fig. 8: Joining individual components

10. Specify finished products

The construction of buildings usually involves industrially produced finished products in combination with building components made by craftsmen. In the detailing phase, the designer specifies the finished products to be used. He does this by showing the selected finished product in the drawing and clearly stating the designation of the product. In order to avoid mistakes, it is advisable to use the same wording as the manufacturer unless it is a requirement for the design and specification to be product-neutral.

SPECIFIC REQUIREMENTS

In addition to the general requirements there is a whole range of specific requirements that must be satisfied by a good detail drawing. As a rule, detail drawings represent the most detailed level of the design and contain the most information. Likewise, the sum of all known specific requirements is greatest at the detailing stage.

Specific requirements typically result from the:

- design intention
- building code/building regulations
- conditions imposed by the planning permission
- fire protection
- structural calculations
- thermal insulation
- sound insulation
- mechanical services
- working drawings/separate details

- technical rules of execution
- user requirements
- costs

TIMING WITHIN THE DESIGN PROCESS

In the best-case scenario, the detail drawings are produced during the same phase in the design process as the working drawings. Frequently, questions arise during the production of working drawings that require detailed investigation. Any findings resulting from careful detailing must be incorporated in the drawings produced in the previous design phases.

It may also be the case that the building is already under construction and a certain detail, for which no drawing has been produced as yet, is unclear and therefore needs to be examined and clarified in a detail drawing. In such a case, there may be parts of the building that have already been constructed, or decisions made that can no longer be changed; therefore the detail drawing must be adapted to achieve the desired result without changing the given parameters.

WORK PROCESSES

The work processes employed in the production of detail drawings are largely the same as those used for the scheme design and working drawings. However, in view of the fact that detail drawings often definitively specify certain parts at a large scale, a structured working approach is particularly important.

When producing a detail drawing, it is helpful to visualize the actual production process in its detailed sequences and to develop the drawing accordingly. This means that, during the design process, one has to ask oneself, 'What comes first, how is it carried out, and what comes next?'

When it is necessary to produce a detail drawing in several steps, a division into shell construction components and fitting-out components may offer a suitable solution. When a detail drawing would be very complex, it may make sense to subdivide the drawing in accordance with the working steps of the different trades since this also reflects the real-life construction process. In that situation it is imperative to ensure that every detail of a work section has been entered completely before the next step follows.

● **Example:** In some cases, the detail design of the joint between a flat roof and a vertical part, such as an elevator bulkhead, leads to the recognition that the vertical face of the bulkhead must be taller.

Components of Detail Drawings

The following chapter covers the most important elements in a technical drawing, that is, lines, hatching, dimensions, and annotations. To a large extent, the same rules apply to detail drawings as to general construction drawings. However, there are a few special rules that should be observed when producing detail drawings. For this reason, this chapter does not focus on the basics of technical drawing but on the special rules
○ that apply to the drawing of details.

LINES

As with all technical drawings, the rule applies that the delimitation of section areas and visible edges of building components are represented by solid lines in detail drawings. Concealed building component edges are shown as dashed lines, and edges located behind the plane of the section as dotted lines. Dash-and-dot lines are used for identifying section planes and axes of building components.

Line weight   ISO 128-23 (Technical Drawings; General Principles of Presentation; Lines on Construction Drawings) and DIN 1356-1 (Building and Civil Engineering Drawings; Types, Content and General Rules for Representation) contain general provisions for the line weight in construction drawings. Certain line groups are allocated to different drawing scales, listing the line weights. > Tab. 1

Tab. 1: Line weights in accordance with DIN 1356-1

	Type of line	Application area	Line group			
			I	II	III	IV
			≤ 1:100		≥ 1:50	
			Line width in mm			
1	Solid line	Delimitation of sectional areas	0.5	**0.5**	**1.0**	1.0
2	Solid line	Visible edges and visible contours of building components, delimitations of sectional areas of narrow or small building components	0.25	**0.35**	**0.5**	0.7
3	Solid line	Dimension lines, extension lines, leader lines, walking lines, delimitation of the edges of detail areas, simplified illustrations	0.18	**0.25**	**0.35**	0.5
4	Dashed line	Concealed edges and concealed contours of building components	0.25	**0.35**	**0.5**	0.7
5	Dash-and-dot line	Identification of the position of the section plane	0.5	**0.5**	**1.0**	1.0
6	Dash-and-dot line	Axes	0.18	**0.25**	**0.35**	0.5
7	Dotted line	Building components behind or above the section plane	0.25	**0.35**	**0.5**	0.7
8	Dimension figures	Font size	2.5	**3.5**	**3.5**	7.0

solid line 0.35 mm – delineation of section areas

solid line 0.25 mm   visible edges and outlines

solid line 0.18 mm – dimension lines, hatching

dashed line 0.18 mm – concealed edges

dotted line 0.18 mm – edges behind the section level

gray line 0.13 mm – outline edges in the background

Fig. 9: Lines

Line groups II and III are the main groups, and line groups I and IV are only used when it is expected that the drawing will subsequently be reduced or enlarged. This information primarily applies to line weights used in drawings produced manually. They should be considered as a guideline only when CAD programs and high-resolution printers are used. In order to improve the general clarity of detail drawings with high information content, it may be advantageous to use thinner lines. > Fig. 9 If in doubt, one should make several test prints at the beginning of the drawing work in order to check the appearance of the drawing.

HATCHING

Hatching is used to improve the legibility and unify the presentation of sectional areas in layout and section drawings. Generally speaking, a distinction is made between hatching that is independent of the material and hatching that is specific to certain materials.

Hatching that is independent of the material is usually diagonal at an angle of 45° that fills the area to be identified.

Hatching that identifies specific materials is defined in DIN ISO 128-50. > Fig. 10

○ **Note:** The *Basics – Technical Drawing* volume by Bert Bielefeld and Isabella Skiba contains a compact account of how to develop construction drawings in different project phases.

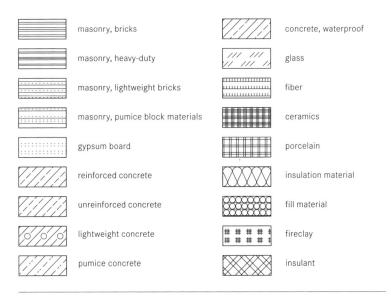

Fig. 10: Hatching for sectional areas in accordance with DIN ISO 128-50

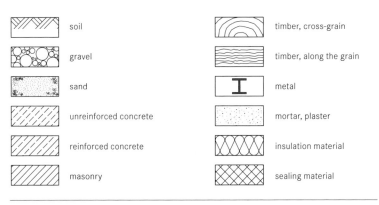

Fig. 11: Identification of sectional areas in accordance with DIN 1356-1/Table 8

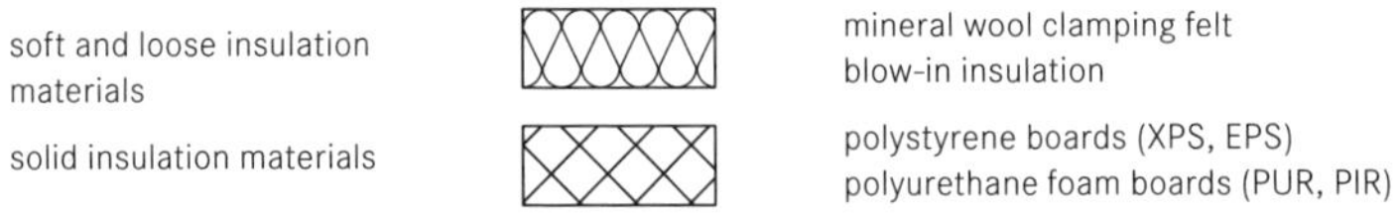

soft and loose insulation materials — mineral wool clamping felt / blow-in insulation

solid insulation materials — polystyrene boards (XPS, EPS) / polyurethane foam boards (PUR, PIR)

Fig. 12: Examples of hatching for different insulation materials

DIN 1356-1 contains typical hatching for specific materials in construction drawings. > Fig. 11

Upon close examination, a contradiction between the standards can be detected – the hatching for unreinforced concrete is shown in DIN ISO 128-50 as solid lines at a 45° angle alternating with two dashed lines at a 45° angle. In DIN 1356 the hatching for unreinforced concrete is shown as a series of dashed lines at a 45° angle. In practice, the hatching shown in DIN 1356 has been widely adopted.

In addition to the above definitions, a distinction between rigid insulating materials in the form of boards (mainly EPS or XPS insulating board) and soft or loose insulating materials (such as mineral wool clamping felt or blow-in insulation) has been widely accepted. > Fig. 12

In view of the many different materials available, it is occasionally necessary to add to the above hatchings or modify them in order to obtain more options. In addition to the general graphic identification of materials via hatching, it is necessary to include the exact designation of the materials in written form. This is generally done by adding annotations.

In addition, it makes sense to list all types of hatching used in the drawing in a plan legend and, if appropriate, to add explanatory text. > Fig. 13 and Chapter Choice of Medium

A general rule on the drawing of hatching is that the lines must be significantly thinner than the delimitation lines. When using a CAD drawing program, the most common line widths for detail drawings is 0.18 mm or 0.13 mm.

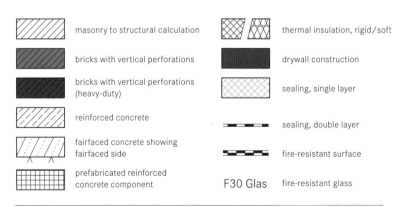

masonry to structural calculation

bricks with vertical perforations

bricks with vertical perforations (heavy-duty)

reinforced concrete

fairfaced concrete showing fairfaced side

prefabricated reinforced concrete component

thermal insulation, rigid/soft

drywall construction

sealing, single layer

sealing, double layer

fire-resistant surface

F30 Glas fire-resistant glass

Fig. 13: Example of hatching symbols with legend

When a section of two building components of the same material is shown, the same hatching is used for both components. Sometimes detail drawings show two different objects adjacent to each other which, although they consist of the same material, must be installed as separate objects (for example, tapered insulation panels placed on base insulation panels). In this case the edges of the panels are drawn as solid lines and the hatching of the one object is applied offset from that of the other object. > Fig. 14

Where hatching needs to be applied to large sectional areas (for example, sections through ground) it is customary, for reasons of clarity, to only enter the hatching along the contour line of the sectional area. For better legibility it is usually helpful to omit any hatching that would cover dimension figures and/or annotations. > Fig. 15

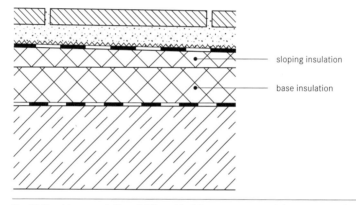

sloping insulation

base insulation

Fig. 14: Graphic presentation of different building components of the same material

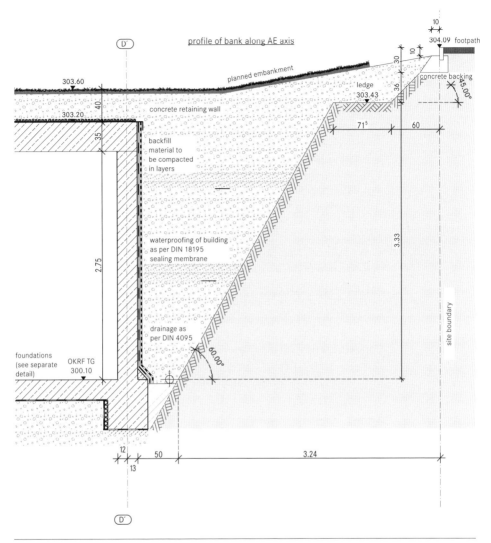

Fig. 15: Example of hatching for large sectional areas

PATTERN LINES

It is common to use symbols for various materials in detail drawings. The most common symbol used is that for sealing membranes, which are represented by a linear pattern with alternating black and white filling between two lines. > Fig. 16

Most CAD programs have predefined pattern lines, which makes entering them significantly easier than in a manual drawing. In addition to varying the height of the pattern lines and the length of the alternating infill, it is also possible to modify them in various other ways in order to represent different membrane materials. So as to avoid confusion, the respective building components should also be identified with annotations. > Fig. 17

It is in the nature of membranes such as sealing membranes, vapor barriers, and especially separating layers that they are significantly thinner than can be shown by the pattern line. For this reason the pattern lines are considered symbols that do not allow any conclusion as to the true thickness of the material. As a general rule, the thickness of membranes is not indicated as part of the dimension line but is stated in the annotations.

When drawing a building component consisting of several layers, it is usual to first draw all the layers of material with their respective thickness and then to add the pattern lines symbolizing the membranes. The real material thickness of membranes less than 5 mm thick (such as vapor barriers and separating layers) is generally discounted in the detail drawing. Where thicker membranes are used (for example, sealing layers) it is important to remember that the overall thickness is doubled in

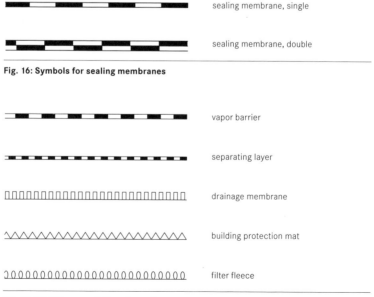

sealing membrane, single

sealing membrane, double

Fig. 16: Symbols for sealing membranes

vapor barrier

separating layer

drainage membrane

building protection mat

filter fleece

Fig. 17: Graphic presentation of membranes

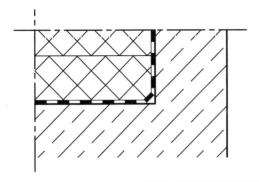

Fig. 18: The hatching of the sectional area does not cover the pattern line

the area of the overlap. In the context of materials and material thickness, an attempt is also made to represent the deformation characteristics of the component in the graphic representation.

For the sake of the clarity of the drawing, it is advisable to omit any hatching in the area of the pattern line. > Fig. 18

INSERTING DIMENSIONS

Dimensions are a particularly important element in construction drawings. Great care must be taken to insert all necessary dimensions accurately. As mentioned at the beginning, it can be helpful to insert the dimension lines directly after drawing an individual element rather than entering all dimensions once the drawing of all components has been completed. Decisions made in the process of producing the drawing, such as the dimensions of an individual part and the distance of that part from another part, are the most important elements of dimensioning.

For the purpose of entering dimensions in detail drawings, dimension chains are used as they are used elsewhere in the construction industry. The components of a dimension chain are: dimension line, extension lines, dimension demarcations, dimension figures, and, if applicable, additional dimension figures to indicate the height of the building component.

The dimension line is a straight solid line that runs parallel to the drawn object to which it relates.

The extension line is a connection line between the element to which the dimension relates and the respective dimension line. However, usually the extension line is shortened in the drawing.

The dimension demarcation marks the beginning and end of a dimension between the intersections of the extension lines with the dimension line. In the construction industry, a common denotation of the dimension demarcation is a short angled line drawn at an angle of 45° to the dimension line, from bottom left to top right. The respective standard (DIN 406) specifies the length of the dimension demarcation line as twelve times

Components of
a dimension chain

the width of the dimension line. A realistic value is 2.5 or 3 mm, which is the standard setting in most CAD programs for all dimension chains.

In addition, it is customary to place the dimension figure above the dimension line rather than interrupting the dimension line. Where it is important to state the height of a building component (for example, a window opening), the dimension of that component is shown beneath the dimension line. > Fig. 19

In technical drawings for steel construction and mechanical engineering, different dimensioning symbols are used. The most frequent symbol is an arrow with the point filled in. In addition, the extension lines are mostly extended up to the object to which the dimension relates, and the unit of measure is millimeters. > Fig. 20

Definition of units of measure In construction drawings it is customary to use meters and centimeters as units of measure. Meters are shown as integral numbers followed by a decimal separator and two digits for centimeters. The decimal separators used vary according to country; in Germany and most countries in Europe and South America, a comma is used; in the English-speaking countries, a full stop.

All measures that are less than 1 m are shown in centimeters without any decimal separator. Units that are smaller than 1 cm are usually rounded to 5 mm and added as a superscript to the centimeter figure.

However, stating dimensions in meters and centimeters is often too imprecise and therefore not customarily used in large-scale detail drawings. Likewise, it is possible that rounding dimensions to the nearest 5 mm step is not precise enough for detail drawings.

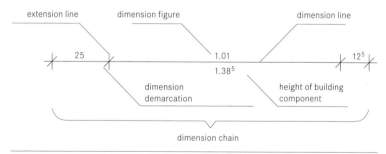

Fig. 19: **Components of a dimension chain for construction drawings**

Fig. 20: **Dimension chain in mechanical engineering drawings**

For this reason, the dimensions on detail drawings are often shown in millimeters. Since this is a deviation from the unit of measure customary in construction drawings, an annotation referring to the unit of measure used should be included in the drawing title block.

In detail drawings that include components in classic masonry dimensions as well as more detailed components such as steel construction parts, it is also possible to use both units of measure in the same drawing. In such a case, the suffix 'cm' or 'mm' is added behind every dimension figure even though the unit of measure of that dimension may be obvious. The advantage of using both units of measure is that common dimensions can be more easily recognized; an example is the classic thickness of a brickwork wall (in Germany, 24 cm) which colloquially may be referred to as a '24 cm wall.'

As mentioned at the beginning of this chapter, the dimensions of each individual element of a detail and the distance between these elements are the critical dimensional criteria. A general rule for entering dimensions on construction drawings is that all dimensions required for producing the object shown must be stated. Irrespective of the fact that drawings are drawn to scale before they are printed out, it is not permissible to measure dimensions with a scale rule off the drawing because this is too imprecise.

Selection of points delimiting a dimension

For the benefit of legibility of drawings, one should ensure that duplications are avoided as much as possible. This applies in particular to detail drawings in which, sometimes, many dimensions have to be entered in little space. In the best case each dimension is only shown once.

In view of the fact that detail drawings carry much information for the joining and processing of building components, it is also important to show the respective dimensions. For example, this may refer to the dimension of the overlap of two building components or the finished height of a building component above another fitting-out component.

Often, the reason for entering such dimensions is that they are governed by certain rules of technology. All dimensions required because of rules in a statutory instrument have to be entered in the drawing. Common dimensions of this type are:

— height of terrain above finished floor level
— clear distances between the balusters of balustrades
— finished sill height above finished floor level
— clear dimensions of door/window openings
— height of door thresholds
— height of the upstand of a sealing membrane at a vertical building component
— height of a plinth above finished ground level
— minimum thickness of insulation material
— rise height, going, and nosing of finished staircases

- height of handrail above staircase finish
- overlap of metal sheeting, profiles, and the overhang of windowsills
- cross sections of ventilation ducts

Other important dimensions for the processing of individual parts include:

- central axes
- fastening axes
- position of drill holes
- hole diameters
- radii of concave profiles
- angles of incline
- fall/slope

Axes and centers are drawn using dash-and-dot lines, and dimensions are entered to these lines. If axes cross over, and when indicating center points, it is important to ensure that the crossing point lies in the dash of the dash-and-dot line so that a cross indicates the respective point.

The dimensions of rectangular cross sections (for example, timber rafters) can also be indicated in the form of a fraction, for example 12/20 (12 wide/20 high). The position of drill hole center points is indicated as a dimension from the center point to the nearest body edge in horizontal and vertical directions.

Diameter dimensions are shown by entering the Ø symbol in front of the dimension figure. The dimensions of radii are shown alongside arrows that are drawn up to the line of the circle, either inside or outside. The letter *R* precedes the dimension figure. > Fig. 21

Angles of inclination are shown either directly in the drawing with a curved angle measuring line and the figure, or separately in a written annotation. The ° symbol follows the dimension figure.

The slope of surfaces is stated in the written annotation and also indicated by an arrow in the direction of the fall. The % symbol follows the dimension figure.

Dimensions in detail drawings

In detail drawings it is preferable to place the dimension lines in direct proximity to the drawn object rather than as a dimension chain at the edge of the drawing as is customary in 1:50 working drawings. This helps to avoid a mix-up of reference points, particularly where these are close together in small component.

The distance between the dimension line and the edge of the drawn component can be assumed to be about 10 mm. The distance between parallel dimension lines should be uniform and be between 6 and 8 mm. In certain situations it is possible to improve the legibility of the dimension lines by drawing the extension lines right up to the point to which

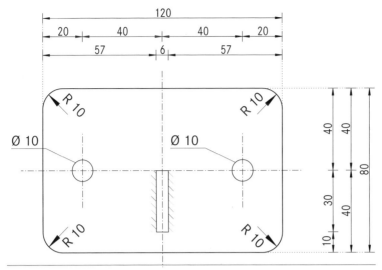

Fig. 21: Dimensions shown in a metal construction drawing

they refer. When extending the extension lines in that way, it is important to ensure that they do not cross over any other dimension line.

Generally, dimension chains should be arranged such that the chain with the smallest dimensions is closest to the object, and the line with the overall dimension is furthest away from the object. Often it is not possible to avoid placing dimension figures on hatched or filled areas. In this case, the dimension figure should be backed by a neutral fill area. The distinction between the dimension lines and the drawn elements is primarily made with the weight of the line. In view of the fact that technical drawings are mostly produced with CAD programs and are printed out by high-resolution plotters, dimension lines measuring 0.18 mm or 0.13 mm are clearly legible and distinct from the heavier lines of component edges. > Fig. 22

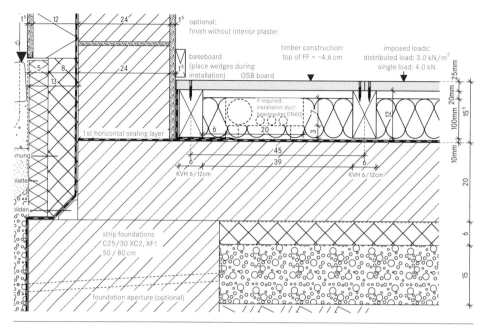

Within the figure, the following labels are visible:

optional:
finish without interior plaster

baseboard
(place wedges during
installation)

timber construction:
top of FF = −4.6 cm
OSB board

imposed loads:
distributed load: 3.0 kN/m²
single load: 4.0 kN

if required:
installation duct
(wastewater DN60)

1st horizontal sealing layer

KVH 6/12cm

KVH 6/12cm

strip foundations
C25/30 XC2, XF1
50/80 cm

foundation aperture (optional)

Dimensions: 12, 24, 1⁵, 5, 8, 24, 13, 6, 20, 45, 39, 6, 25mm, 20mm, 100mm, 15⁵, 10mm, 20, 6, 15

Fig. 22: Dimensions in detail construction drawings

ANNOTATIONS

Annotations are particularly important in detail drawings because they often contain many individual parts which require further explanation in addition to the drawn illustration. Furthermore, many material properties and processing methods cannot be fully explained by drawing; therefore annotations are important. > Fig. 23

Designation of
individual parts

The most important part of the annotation is the designation of all individual parts of a construction. This helps to avoid misunderstandings in the interpretation of the content of drawings and to explain the meaning of hatching patterns. The designation of such parts should be short, concise, and commonly understood, referring to the individual part shown and including some reference to the type of material, for example, 'reinforced concrete floor.'

Reference to
information from
specialist engineers

For components which are subject to the design input of specialist engineers, such as a structural engineer, it is recommended to add a reference in the annotation, for example, 'reinforced concrete floor in accordance with structural calculations.'

Description of
individual parts

In addition to the designation of the individual part, those properties of the part should be described that are necessary or required from a construction, design, or functional point of view. In view of the fact that these properties often cannot be expressed in the drawing, a mention of the respective property in the annotations is mandatory, for example, 're-

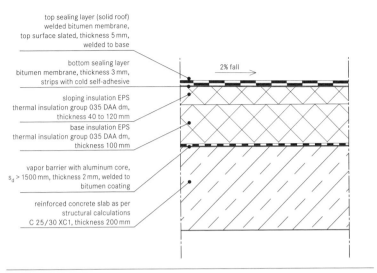

top sealing layer (solid roof)
welded bitumen membrane,
top surface slated, thickness 5 mm,
welded to base

bottom sealing layer
bitumen membrane, thickness 3 mm,
strips with cold self-adhesive

2% fall

sloping insulation EPS
thermal insulation group 035 DAA dm,
thickness 40 to 120 mm

base insulation EPS
thermal insulation group 035 DAA dm,
thickness 100 mm

vapor barrier with aluminum core,
s_d > 1500 mm, thickness 2 mm, welded to
bitumen coating

reinforced concrete slab as per
structural calculations
C 25/30 XC1, thickness 200 mm

Fig. 23: Product-neutral annotations, including material properties

inforced concrete floor in accordance with structural calculations, C 30/37 XC3, resistant to deicing agents.'

In cases where further processing of the planned component is intended, this must be mentioned in the annotations and detailed as precisely as possible. Again, this is necessary because usually this type of information cannot be expressed in the drawing. For example: 'reinforced concrete floor in accordance with structural calculations, C 30/37 XC3, resistant to deicing agents, top face smoothed with mechanical trowel, R10.'

Examples of some frequently listed properties:

Processing of individual parts

— Coated
— Galvanized
— Ground
— Polished
— Painted
— Oiled
— Lacquered
— Dyed
— Smoothed
— Textured
— Satin-finished

- Rough-sawn
- Bush-hammered
- Flamed
- Sandblasted
- Corrugated
- Broken

Stating the dimension

In addition to the dimension in the drawing, important measurements of individual parts are also stated in the annotations. For reasons of legibility, it is important to ensure that the selected unit of measure is the same as that in the dimension lines, for example, 'reinforced concrete floor in accordance with structural calculations, C 30/37 XC3, resistant to deicing agents, top face smoothed with mechanical trowel R10, thickness = 240 mm.'

Joining method

Depending on the building component, the method used to join it with other components can be of critical importance. Therefore the annotations should include a statement in this respect. This is particularly important when the method of joining cannot be illustrated in the drawing. For example: 'top sealing layer in welded elastomeric bitumen, top surface slated, thickness = 5 mm, welded to base.'

Examples of common joining methods:

- Screwed
- Welded
- Soldered
- Bonded
- Pointed (with mortar)
- Filled
- Self-adhesive
- Riveted
- Nailed
- Clamped
- Push-fitted
- Wedged
- Dovetailed
- Butt-jointed
- Rebated
- Overlapping
- Unrestrained
- Under imposed load
- Unrestrained
- Nonexpanding

In cases in which finished products have to be modified, or their properties specified in greater detail, it is useful to clearly point out these requirements. This can be done using annotations in addition to the drawn object, for example, 'Modification: connection plate 100 mm in length instead of 60 mm.'

Modification of finished products

In many cases, products made by various manufacturers are available on the market for a specific application. In order to ensure that the design is as universally applicable as possible, it makes sense to add 'or equivalent' to the annotation referring to the product. For the contractor, this means that another product with equivalent properties can also be used.

For example, many products by different manufacturers are available where the annotation says 'top sealing membrane for flat roofs.' In this case, the annotation could be: 'top sealing layer in welded elastomeric bitumen, top surface slated, welded to base, for example, *MANUFACTURER XY, PRODUCT XY* or equivalent.'

In order to ensure that the detail drawings are properly referenced within the design documentation, and to ensure that it is easy to see which parts are shown in more detailed drawings, references to details are included in the 1:50 scale working drawings. The symbols used for this depend on personal preference, but should be consistent within a project. The text of the reference can be relatively short, usually stating the designation of the detail, the respective drawing number, and the scale selected. > Fig. 24

References to details

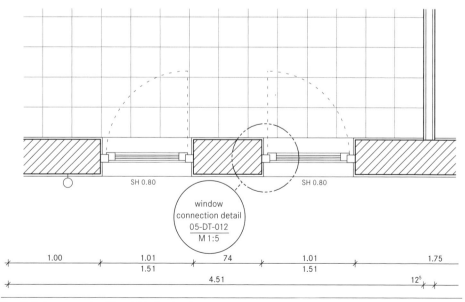

Fig. 24: Reference to detail in a 1:50 plan drawing

The same or a similar method should be used to refer to any detail drawings by third-party stakeholders in the project such as structural engineers or services engineers. In cases where calculations have been produced for the purpose of providing separate evidence, it makes sense to include a reference to these in the working drawings.

ANNOTATION SYSTEMS

The annotations in detail drawings can be entered using a range of different systems which depend on the object illustrated, the information to be conveyed, and personal preference. However, within a project, the style of the annotations should be kept consistent.

References to details
When detail drawings are produced with many individual elements and a high proportion of information in the form of annotations, it is recommended to use number references and text blocks. Given that a detail drawing consisting of many different elements is fairly complex anyway, the advantage of this is that the drawing itself is not cluttered by the text and yet reference to the text is ensured via the reference numbers.

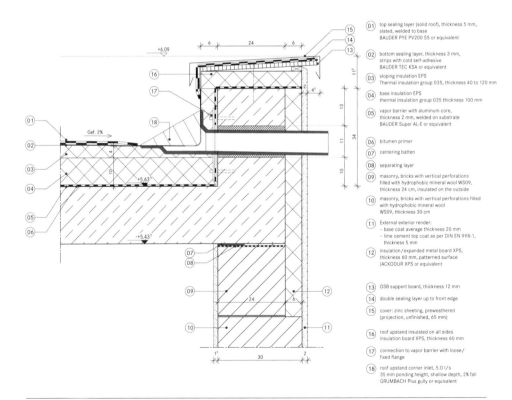

Fig. 25: Annotations with number references and text blocks on the side of the drawing

34

In addition, it is easier to extend the text block on the side of the drawing with additional entries. The disadvantage of the system with number references is that the user of the drawing has to switch between the drawing and the list of annotations. > Fig. 25

When annotations are inserted close to the drawing, text pointers can be used to identify individual elements. It is usual to use lines or arrows to assign text to the respective object. In this case it is important to ensure that the lines of the text pointers can be clearly distinguished from the lines defining the object. It is also beneficial for the legibility of the drawing when the lines of the text pointers are not angled more than once. The advantage of this system is that the drawn elements can be simply and quickly identified from the adjacent text. However, in drawings with a great number of details, this system may be confusing if there is insufficient space to accommodate all the annotations in a clear manner. The text blocks should be right- or left-aligned, and the line spacing between them should be uniform. If information is added at a later date, it may be necessary to rearrange the layout of the text blocks and adjust the lines. > Fig. 26

> Text pointers

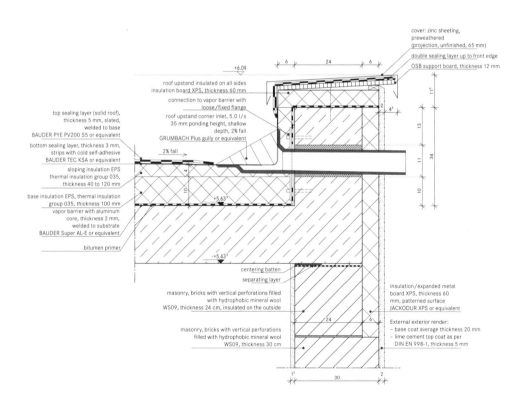

Fig. 26: Annotations with text pointers to individual parts

Another option for annotations in detail drawings is the use of text pointers and composite text blocks for building elements consisting of several layers. For example, it is possible to describe a flat roof, floor construction, or facade construction using a composite text block while other individual elements are explained using text with a text pointer. The advantage is that the explanation of the construction of the element can be kept separate from the actual drawing, thus leaving sufficient space for the explanation of individual items. > Fig. 27

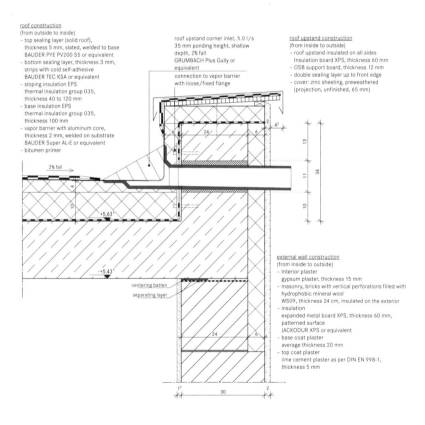

roof construction
(from outside to inside)
- top sealing layer (solid roof),
  thickness 5 mm, slated, welded to base
  BAUDER PYE PV200 S5 or equivalent
- bottom sealing layer, thickness 3 mm,
  strips with cold self-adhesive
  BAUDER TEC KSA or equivalent
- sloping insulation EPS
  thermal insulation group 035,
  thickness 40 to 120 mm
- base insulation EPS
  thermal insulation group 035,
  thickness 100 mm
- vapor barrier with aluminum core,
  thickness 2 mm, welded on substrate
  BAUDER Super AL-E or equivalent
- bitumen primer

2% fall

+5.63

+5.43

centering batten

separating layer

roof upstand corner inlet, 5.0 l/s
35 mm ponding height, shallow
depth, 2% fall
GRUMBACH Plus Gully or
equivalent
connection to vapor barrier
with loose/fixed flange

roof upstand construction
(from inside to outside)
- roof upstand insulated on all sides
  Insulation board XPS, thickness 60 mm
- OSB support board, thickness 12 mm
- double sealing layer up to front edge
- cover: zinc sheeting, preweathered
  (projection, unfinished, 65 mm)

external wall construction
(from inside to outside)
- Interior plaster
  gypsum plaster, thickness 15 mm
- masonry, bricks with vertical perforations filled with
  hydrophobic mineral wool
  WS09, thickness 24 cm, insulated on the exterior
- insulation
  expanded metal board XPS, thickness 60 mm,
  patterned surface
  JACKODUR XPS or equivalent
- base coat plaster
  average thickness 20 mm
- top coat plaster
  lime cement plaster as per DIN EN 998-1,
  thickness 5 mm

Fig. 27: Annotations with text blocks for standard details, and text pointers for individual items

Preparation

In preparation for a detail drawing, some basic decisions have to be made – from the choice of objects to be illustrated in the drawing to the form and the scale of the illustration.

SELECTION OF AREA TO BE DETAILED

The selection of objects to be illustrated in detail varies from project to project, and is essentially governed by the following criteria:

— The purpose of the drawing
— The complexity of the planned building
— The uniqueness of the construction
— Specific questions raised during the working drawings phase

Fundamentally, all building components that have a special shape and are complicated to produce (interaction between many individual elements/trades) should be carefully detailed. This reduces the number of queries from executing companies and, furthermore, is useful for checking the feasibility of the respective item in the overall context of the design. By contrast, components which are largely defined by the generally recognized rules of technology are not normally shown in detail. For example, to explain the construction of a standard external wall, it is sufficient to show the element in the working drawing at a scale of 1:50 and to add a description of the construction in the form of an annotation. However, it is possible that the junction between the floor slab and the external brickwork has to meet special requirements (for example, specific structural or thermal insulation details). In that case it makes sense to produce a detail drawing of the junction between the floor slab and the external wall construction.

In building projects, details are frequently produced for the following areas:

Typical details

Foundations:
— Actual foundations
— Drainage
— Damp-proofing details

Facade:
— Window and external door connections
— Transitions between soil and vertical components
— Connections between facade and roof
— Junctions of floor/ceiling slabs

- Corner situations
- Balconies
- Parapets
- Solar screening and glare protection
- Barrier-free doors

Roof:
- Flat roof/pitched roof construction
- Roof upstand
- Eaves
- Ridge
- Verge
- Roof penetrations such as chimneys
- Dome lights and rooflights

Staircases:
- Top and bottom joining details
- Landings
- Railings

Floor construction:
- Structural floor construction
- Tile finishes
- Transitions between different floor finishes
- Junctions between floors and vertical elements and openings
- Penetrations

Doors:
- System doors
- Frame systems
- Access flaps to ducts

Drywall construction:
- Connections between walls, floors, and ceilings
- Bulkheads
- Suspended ceilings
- Wall recesses

Fitted items:
- Kitchens
- Fitted furniture
- Technical installations
- Pipe penetrations

FORMS OF REPRESENTATION

Generally, details are drawn using the views customary in construction drawings:

— Vertical section: The most frequently used representation for detail drawings is the vertical section, since this can convey particularly large amounts of information on the connection between individual components. > Fig. 28

— Horizontal section/plan: It may also make sense to show the detail in a horizontal section or plan, depending on the area to be detailed. In view of the fact that the term *plan* is mostly associated with the plan layout of buildings or rooms, it is usual to use the term *horizontal section* for technical detail drawings. Both terms refer to the same method of illustration. > Fig. 29

   However, in contrast to the scheme design and working drawings at a scale of 1:50, where the notional horizontal level is usually 1.00 m above floor level, the level of the horizontal section in detail drawings depends on the particular information intended to be shown for the object to be illustrated.

— Elevation drawings: The horizontal and vertical section drawings of a detail are often supplemented by one or several elevation drawings (for example, outside and inside elevations) in order to round off the illustration in all three dimensions. > Fig. 30

Depending on the complexity of the detail, it may be appropriate – or necessary – to add further illustrations. Typical forms of illustration in detail design include:

— Isometric drawing: Isometric drawings are used to illustrate the context of components including corner details. An isometric is often an additional, simplified illustration. > Fig. 31

— Exploded view drawing: This form of isometric drawing is used to show the individual parts of a complex detail in an exploded view. This makes it possible to clarify how the individual parts fit and function together. > Fig. 32

— Detail collage: For the purpose of illustration it may be useful to show several details at the same scale together in an additional, larger drawing in the correct position in relation to one another. For example, the details of the foundations, the bottom and top window connections, the junction of the roof slab, and the eaves and ridge details in one conjoined illustration provide a section through the building with detailed information content. > Fig. 33

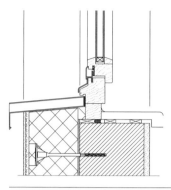

Fig. 28: Vertical section in a detail drawing

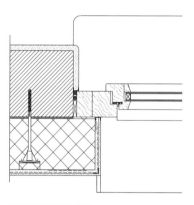

Fig. 29: Horizontal section in a detail drawing

Fig. 30: External elevation of detail

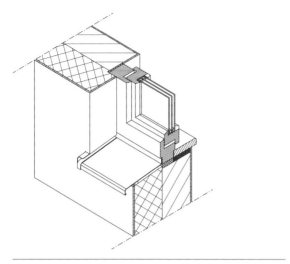

Fig. 31: Isometric detail drawing

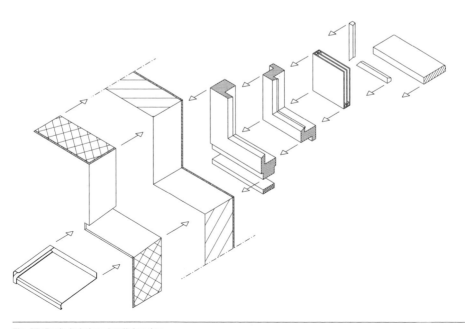

Fig. 32: Exploded view detail drawing

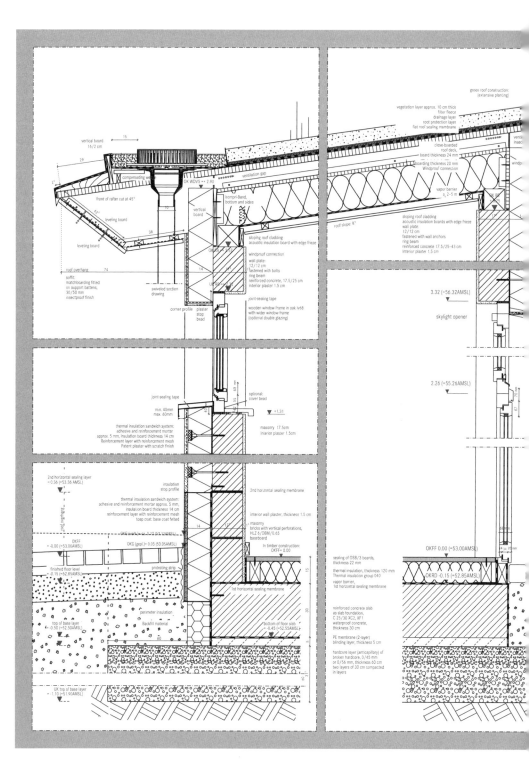

green roof construction:
(extensive planting)

vegetation layer approx. 10 cm thick
filter fleece
drainage layer
root protection layer
flat roof sealing membrane

close-boarded
roof deck,
board thickness 24 mm
boarding thickness 20 mm
Windproof connection

vertical board
16/2 cm

15

29

compensating w...

OK WDVS = 2.90

ventilation gap

front of rafter cut at 45°

vertical
board

kompri-Band,
bottom and sides

windpro...
insec...

venti...

vapor barrier
4, 2-5 m

leveling board

roof slope: 8°

sloping roof cladding
acoustic insulation boards with edge frieze
wall plate:
12/12 cm
fastened with wall anchors
ring beam
reinforced concrete 17.5/25-43 cm
interior plaster 1.5 cm

leveling board

sloping roof cladding
acoustic insulation board with edge frieze

windproof connection
wall plate:
12/12 cm
fastened with bolts
ring beam
reinforced concrete, 17.5/25 cm
interior plaster 1.5 cm

roof overhang   74

soffit:
matchboarding fitted
on support battens,
30/50 mm
insectproof finish

swiveled section
drawing

corner profile   plaster
                 stop
                 bead

joint-sealing tape

wooden window frame in oak iv68
with wider window frame
(optional double glazing)

3.32 (=56.32AMSL)

skylight opener

joint-sealing tape

optional:
cover bead

min. 40mm
max. 60mm

▼ +1.31

masonry 17.5cm
interior plaster 1.5cm

2.26 (=55.26AMSL)

thermal insulation sandwich system:
adhesive and reinforcement mortar
approx. 5 mm, insulation board thickness 14 cm
Reinforcement layer with reinforcement mesh
Patent plaster with scratch finish

2nd horizontal sealing layer
= 0.36 (=53.36 AMSL)

insulation
stop profile

2nd horizontal sealing membrane

thermal insulation sandwich system:
adhesive and reinforcement mortar approx. 5 mm,
insulation board thickness 14 cm
reinforcement layer with reinforcement mesh
toap coat: base coat felted

interior wall plaster, thickness 1.5 cm

masonry
bricks with vertical perforations,
HLZ 6/OBM/0.65
baseboard

In timber construction:
OKFF= 0.00

OKFF
= -0.00 (=53.00AMSL)

OKG (geol.)= 0.05 (53.05AMSL)

OKFF 0.00 (=53.00AMSL)

finished floor level
-0.15 (=52.85AMSL)

protecting strip

sealing of OSB/3 boards,
thickness 22 mm

thermal insulation, thickness 120 mm
Thermal insulation group 040
vapor barrier,
1st horizontal sealing membrane

OKRD -0.15 (=52.85AMSL)

top of base layer
= -0.50 (=52.50AMSL)

Backfill material

perimeter insulation

1st horizontal sealing membrane

bottom of floor slab
= -0.45 (52.55AMSL)

reinforced concrete slab
as slab foundation,
C 25/30 XC2, XF !
waterproof concrete,
thickness 30 cm

PE membrane (2-layer)
blinding layer, thickness 5 cm

hardcore layer (anticapillary) of
broken hardcore, 0/45 mm
or 0/56 mm, thickness 60 cm
two layers of 30 cm compacted
in layers

UK top of base layer
= -1.10 (=51.90AMSL)

DEFINING THE AREA TO BE REPRESENTED

As mentioned above, the focus of a detail drawing is on how to join individual elements in a construction. For this reason, one should select the area to be illustrated such that the greatest number of details can be shown and explained. It is also important to limit the area such that only one functional context is illustrated and all individual components in that area are taken into account. For reasons of clarity, one should avoid showing the same detail in different drawings. It is advisable to concentrate on one single construction aspect. This means that many drawings are produced during the detail design phase. It may therefore be useful to produce a detail collage in addition to the individual drawing.

SELECTING THE SCALE OF THE DRAWING

In detail drawing, it is common for scales from 1:1 and 1:25 to be used. In accordance with DIN ISO 5455, the scales 1:1, 1:2, 1:5, 1:10, or 1:20 are recommended. These can be supplemented with the scale of 1:25. Should it not be possible, in special cases, to use the recommended scales, it is permissible to use intermediate scales. The scale used in the drawing must be clearly indicated in the drawing title block.

The size and complexity of the smallest individual parts to be illustrated give an indication as to an appropriate drawing scale. For example, this could be a specifically defined screw fixing. When the contours of this individual element can no longer be clearly recognized and distinguished, one should choose a larger drawing scale. The scale and the size of the area to be shown in the drawing together determine the size of the drawing. This in turn determines the paper format.

■ A change of scale means a different level of information

It is true for all construction drawings that a switch to a larger scale does not just mean an enlargement of the object; it also, of necessity, requires additional information input. The content of a drawing, that is, the drawing itself with the dimensioning and annotation, varies according to its scale. > Fig. 34

Omission lines

When showing large objects in detail it makes sense (and is normal) to omit any areas that do not contain much information.

When detailing a window, the main areas of interest are the top and bottom connections with the building fabric. The largest part of the window is taken up by the glazing unit. This has the same cross section

---

■ **Tip:** For reasons of easy handling and copying, the DIN A3 format is usually the preferred format for detail drawings. Larger formats are used for complex details and detail collages.

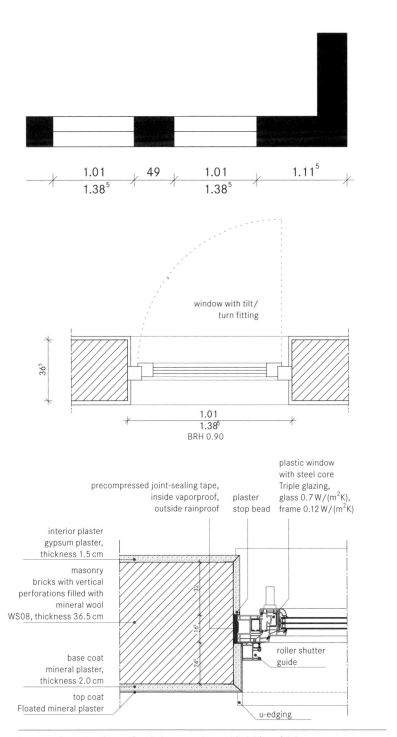

1.01   49   1.01   1.11⁵
1.38⁵   1.38⁵

window with tilt/
turn fitting

36⁵

1.01
1.38⁵
BRH 0.90

plastic window
with steel core
Triple glazing,
glass $0.7\,W/(m^2K)$,
frame $0.12\,W/(m^2K)$

precompressed joint-sealing tape,
inside vaporproof,
outside rainproof

plaster
stop bead

interior plaster
gypsum plaster,
thickness 1.5 cm

masonry
bricks with vertical
perforations filled with
mineral wool
WS08, thickness 36.5 cm

base coat
mineral plaster,
thickness 2.0 cm

top coat
Floated mineral plaster

roller shutter
guide

u-edging

Fig. 34: Information depth of a window at scales 1:100, 1:50, and 1:5

45

throughout its entire height, and therefore is not really important for the purpose of showing relevant details. Therefore, in order to provide drawings with meaningful detail content, it is common practice to omit parts of the object, marking the omission with omission lines and moving the shown parts closer together. If this foreshortening affects a dimension line, the dimension figure must nevertheless show the actual dimension of the object. In this case, a symbol is placed on the dimension line to show that the line was shortened, but the figure nevertheless indicates the true (unshortened) size of the object. > Fig. 35

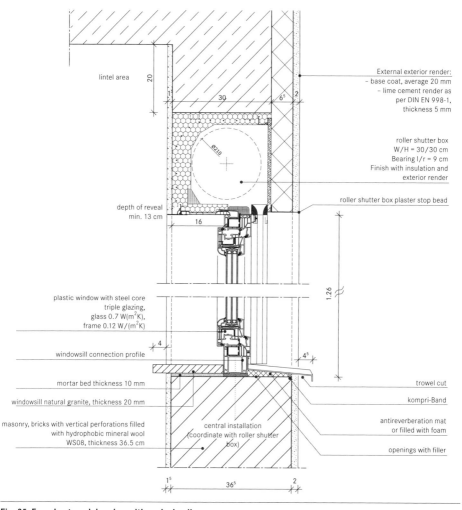

Fig. 35: Foreshortened drawing with omission lines

In rare cases the individual parts to be shown are so small in their Enlargement scale true dimensions that the drawing is produced at an enlarged scale. DIN ISO 5455 recommends the following scales: 2:1, 5:1, 10:1, or 20:1.

When using an enlargement scale, it is usually helpful to also show the illustrated object at its true 1:1 scale. For this purpose, the object is simplified by just showing its contours. > Fig. 36

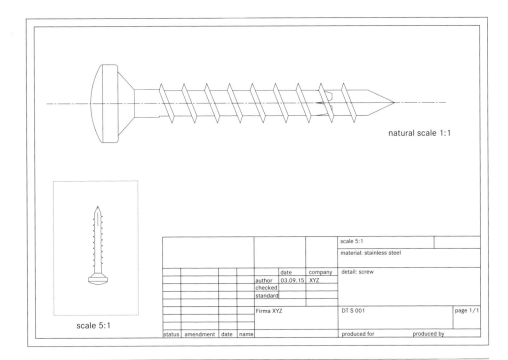

Fig. 36: Enlargement scale drawing

Example of the Process of Producing a Detail Drawing

The example in the following chapter explains how the details mentioned above can be dealt with in the process of producing a detail drawing.

Here, the railing of a balcony is detailed, including the method of fastening it to the building. The drawing is based on information contained in the working drawings, which include a plan and section drawing at a scale of 1:50. > Figs. 37 and 38

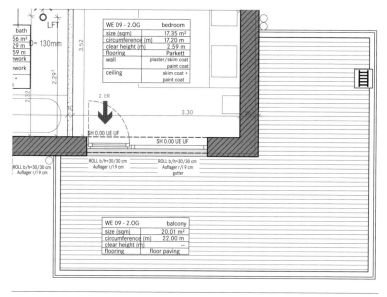

Fig. 37: Part of the layout drawing at a scale of 1:50

○ **Note:** For technical reasons, the drawings in this book are not shown at their proper scale. This change in size may mean that the appearance of parts of the drawing does not fully comply with design principles.

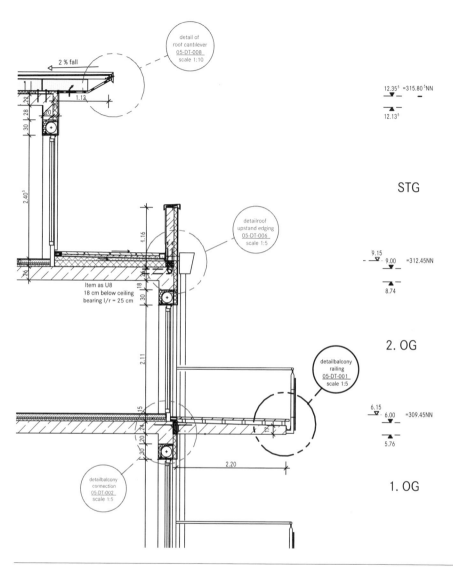

2 % fall

detail of
roof cantilever
05-DT-008
scale 1:10

1.12

2.40⁵

12.35^5 =315.80⁵NN

12.13^5

STG

detailroof
upstand edging
05-DT-006
scale 1:5

1.16

Item as U8
18 cm below ceiling
bearing l/r = 25 cm

9.15
9.00 =312.45NN

8.74

2.11

2. OG

detailbalcony
railing
05-DT-001
scale 1:5

6.15
6.00 =309.45NN

5.76

2.20

detailbalcony
connection
05-DT-002
scale 1:5

1. OG

Fig. 38: Part of the longitudinal section drawing at a scale of 1:50

The balcony railing will contribute significantly to the appearance of the building and is intended to underscore the high quality of the project. For this reason – from the point of view of the conceptual design – it is necessary to show the railing in greater detail. In addition, even if a finished product is used for the balcony railing, it always has to be installed to suit the details of the adjacent building fabric and the installation details should be shown in a drawing.

Furthermore, in most cases a whole host of other requirements need to be considered in the detailing in addition to the conceptual design intent. In the case of the balcony railing, these include the rainwater drainage, the fastening of the railing, and the construction of the balcony itself. The section drawing at a 1:50 scale (> Fig. 38) includes only a little information on these issues, which means that a detailed look at this area is also required from a technical point of view.

The section drawing indicates that rainwater is intended to drain toward the face of the balcony slab and that the gutter is to be fitted between the balcony slab and the railing. The detail drawing is produced to show the exact design and dimensions, and is described below.

As can be seen from the 1:50 drawing, additional areas were identified to be illustrated in detailed form. The respective detail references were marked. What all these areas have in common is that they need to be drawn with special attention to conceptual details and that the technical context of a great number of individual parts has to be designed.

Selecting the area
to be shown in
greater detail

In this example, the focus is on a detailed description of the railing, how it is fastened to the building (in this case to the balcony), and how the rainwater drainage works in the context of the balcony construction. This means that the area to be shown must be selected such that all information relating to this functional context can be shown. This includes the railing itself, its interface with the balcony, the gutter in the space between these two elements, and the balcony construction.

Furthermore, the area should be selected such that details belonging to a different functional context are not included in the drawing but are shown in a separate detail drawing. In this case, the dimensions of the balcony slab and how it connects with the building are shown in the working drawings and in a separate detail drawing. In order to avoid duplication and potential misunderstanding, the area to be shown could be selected as follows. > Fig. 39

The overall size of the area to be shown in the drawing can be computed as follows: 90 cm (railing) + approximately 15 cm (balcony flooring) + 17 cm (balcony slab) = 122 cm. At a scale of 1:5, this corresponds to a drawing size of about 25 cm. At a scale of 1:2, the size of the drawing would be 61 cm high. This means that at this scale the drawing would be too big to fit on DIN A1 paper in landscape format (h = 59.4 × w = 84.1 cm).

To make the drawing fit to the paper size, it would be possible to cut out part of the drawing at a certain place where no information is lost

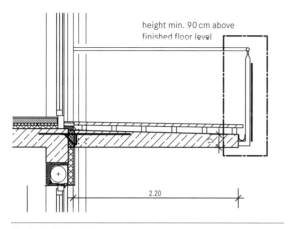

height min. 90 cm above
finished floor level

2.20

Fig. 39: Selection of area to be shown in a detail drawing

(part of the post and glass pane) and to push the upper and lower parts of the drawing together (> Chapter Preparation, Selecting the scale of the drawing). As a result, the overall size of the drawing would be reduced.

When considering the smallest elements of the drawing, it is necessary to anticipate the next steps. The smallest object that needs to be included in the illustration is the combination of screw and anchor between the railing and the balcony slab, which was specified by the structural engineer as an M12 screw with a corresponding heavy-duty anchor. This means that, in the metric system, the screw is 12 mm thick. At the scale of 1:2, this means that the distance between the lines outlining the shaft of the screw is 6 mm, at the scale of 1:5, it is 2.4 mm. When using a line measuring 0.13 mm for the smallest parts, it is therefore possible to show the object clearly at a scale of 1:5.

In this case, for the sake of clarity as well as to be able to show the object in its entirety, the scale of 1:5 was selected for the detail drawing. ○

We now have completed the selection of the details and area to be shown in the detail drawing, and have decided on the scale of the drawing. In the next step, all requirements relating to the building component and the representation of the area to be detailed should be compiled.

○ **Note:** It is also possible to change the scale of the drawing if this seems appropriate after producing a test printout. However, it is important to remember that the information content of the drawing must be adjusted to the changed scale.

Based on the previous chapters, an example of requirements is given for the detailing of this building component:

- 1. Design intention: Railing attached to posts, with handrail placed on tapered post profile. Railing to be fastened to the face of the existing balcony slab. Frosted glass panes as infill and as a means to conceal the drainage gutter and the floor finish.
- 2. Building code / building regulations: Minimum height for fall prevention at heights of less than 10 m: 90 cm from finished floor level (FFL). In this case, the balcony wraps around the building corner and the minimum height must be measured from the most unfavorable point, that is, at the highest point of the balcony floor finish nearest the building.
- 3. Building permission: In this particular case, a condition of the building permission stated that, in terms of minimum distance to other buildings, frosted railing infills are to be considered equivalent to solid walls. This means the minimum distances must be checked accordingly.
- 4. Fire protection: The second rescue route for each apartment is via the balcony. This means that the railing is subject to the imposition of a load at points where ladders can be placed.
- 5. Structural integrity: The height of the posts, the spacing of the posts, and the characteristic lateral pressure exerted by persons leaning against the railing of residential buildings, are input data for producing the structural calculations as evidence of structural integrity. In this case, the following additional loads apply: the solid glass infill is exposed to a certain wind pressure; the glass pane is more than 2 m distant from the building, which means that wind suction must also be taken into account. These loads and the load resulting from a ladder leaning against the railing in a rescue operation are computed by the structural engineer and determine the size of the face plate and the necessary screw fixings.
- 6. Thermal insulation: This requirement does not apply in this case because the thermal separation is inserted between the balcony slab and the building.
- 7. Services installations: The rainwater downpipe can be fitted at either end of the corner balcony where it meets the building.
- 8. Working drawing or separate detail drawing: The balcony slab is thermally separated from the building and consists of a partially finished product in the shape of a trough to be completed on site. The material thickness of the trough is 6 cm and the upstand at the front is 17 cm high and that at the back, closest to the building, is 22 cm high. Reinforcement steel is applied to the hollow area, which is then filled with in situ concrete with the surface sloping toward the front.

— 9. Technical rules of execution: In accordance with DIN 18195 (Waterproofing of Buildings), roof surfaces (and balcony surfaces) accessed by users are to have a minimum fall of 2% if a single layer of waterproofing is applied.
As the balcony is 2.20 m wide, the front is 17 cm high and the back, closest to the building, is 22 cm high, producing a 5 cm fall.
— The required dimensions of the gutter are calculated in accordance with DIN 18460 (External Rainwater Pipes and Eaves Gutters), resulting in a 200 nominal size cross-section.
— 10. User requirements: The building owner and user have a preference for a maximum slope of the finish of 1.5 cm per meter.
— 11. Costs: The number of posts and their height is to be kept as small as possible, taking into account all other necessary requirements. ○

Depending on the detail, individual project characteristics, and special features, the requirements can be very different. For example, in certain details some requirement lists can be omitted completely or be replaced by others. Nevertheless, a systematic listing of all known requirements and their source provides a useful guideline.

The above example demonstrates the many requirements that need to be taken into consideration for just one construction detail. Having compiled this list, all requirements are known and have been researched. If the requirements are all accommodated as part of a thorough detail design, the path has been cleared for a construction design that is correct in accordance with the preparatory work.

As a preliminary step of the detail design using a CAD program, a hand sketch has been produced which captures the construction idea as well as a rough idea of the dimensions. > Fig. 40

Freehand sketch

○ **Note:** All built components are subject to certain manufacturing and processing tolerances. These are defined in DIN 18202 (Tolerances in Building Construction) and are mainly subdivided into the areas of longitudinal deviation, angle deviation, and deviation from flatness. When designing details in which delicate industrially produced finished products are used in combination with manually produced shell building components, it is advisable to allow for the use of packing layers.

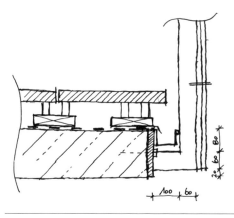

Fig. 40: Freehand sketch based on the construction idea

As a starting point, it is advisable to copy the area covering the detail from the 1:50 working drawing and trim it to the specific area selected for the detail. Then all known details that are not yet included in the 1:50 drawing should be added to the detail design area. In this case these are:

1. Construction of the balcony slab as a partially finished product with a material thickness of 6 cm and an upstand in front of 17 cm and, at the back, closest to the building, of 22 cm.
2. Detailing of the finished component with a weather groove and a 1 cm chamfered edge on the underside.
3. The hollow part is filled with reinforced concrete and finished to a fall of approximately 2%.

The contours are drawn with uninterrupted lines (line measuring 0.35 or 0.25 mm) and the sectional area is filled with hatching indicating the specific material. In this detail the work to be completed by the shell construction trades is to be shown with a grey background in order to identify the interface between shell building and installation. At this stage it is useful, in order to ensure a systematic approach, to start a plan legend for all types of hatching used. This means that the first part of the
■ drawing looks as follows: > Fig. 41

Adding other
known components
In the next step, any other known components of the detail are to be added. Here it is advisable to proceed in the same sequence as will be adopted in the later implementation phase. In this way, the detail design functions as a mental test run for the construction phase. Should this reveal any problems, there is still the opportunity to revise the construction.

In this example, a finished product was selected in the design process which is to be adapted in accordance with the characteristics of the

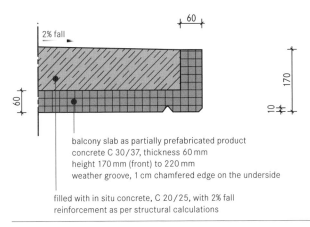

balcony slab as partially prefabricated product
concrete C 30/37, thickness 60 mm
height 170 mm (front) to 220 mm
weather groove, 1 cm chamfered edge on the underside

filled with in situ concrete, C 20/25, with 2% fall
reinforcement as per structural calculations

Fig. 41: First stage of the detail drawing

building and the special technical requirements. The selection of the finished product is meant to make a design statement. In the case that comparable products are also permissible, the annotations should indicate this by adding "or equivalent."

In order to be able to determine the required position, it is necessary to obtain the structural calculations for the fastening and the details of the face plate and edge distances of the holes included in the structural calculations. Early on, the decision was made to place the gutter in the intermediate space between railing and slab; the structural calculations allow for any resulting loads to optimize the detailing.

In this case, the fastening of the railing was specified to consist of a stainless steel face plate measuring 15 × 240 × 160 mm, the latter being the maximum available height at the face of the slab. The two lateral fixings consisting of M 12 screws and heavy-duty anchors are to be inserted with a distance of 90 mm from the lower edge.

■ **Tip**: When producing drawings using a CAD system, it is helpful – at an early stage – to distribute the different components of the drawing to their respective layers. For an individual detail drawing, the minimum division could be as follows:
– Lines (add other building component layers if required)
– Hatching and infill areas
– Dimension chains
– Annotations and pointers

The posts of the railing are welded to the face plate via an L-shaped connecting plate. In accordance with the calculations, the top edge of the horizontal part of the connecting plate can be level with the center of the drill holes. This then leaves enough height for accommodating the gutter.

The structural engineer has produced detailed calculations to prove the structural integrity of the fastening for the railing. The explanations for the calculations cannot be fully included in the detail drawing because there is not enough space, and it would be detrimental to the clarity of the drawing. For this reason, a reference to the structural drawings is included in the annotations.

Now additional parts of the railing are added to the drawing. Joining methods (in this case screw fixings and welded connections) are shown, and fastening axes are entered. In the same work step, the dimensions of the important edges of the added parts are shown. For reasons of clarity, the annotations are added step by step in this example. However, often the annotations are entered separately at a later stage. > Fig. 42

The section drawing cannot be used to show the distance between the railing posts, as this dimension cannot be seen. One option for showing the spacing of the railing posts is to transfer the details established by now back to the 1:50 plan drawing, and to distribute the posts evenly. This establishes the maximum spacing between the railing posts, which is then included in the annotations.

Adding other components

In the next step, the drainage components are entered. In this case these consist of a box gutter, which was calculated to require a dimension of 70 × 42 mm, the gutter holders, and the drip plate. In view of the fact that the gutter is to have a fall, the drawing shows the highest point with a solid section line and the lowest point with a dashed line. This is mainly done to ensure that the fall of the gutter can be accommodated over the length of its run.

In order to make it possible for the gutter to be fitted in the space between the face plate and the railing posts, the length of the horizontal element of the connection plate was increased from the standard 60 mm to 100 mm. An annotation is added to ensure that this modification is not overlooked by subsequent users of the detail drawing, for example, by the checking structural engineer or when materials are ordered.

In anticipation of the next step, the sealing membrane for the balcony surface is entered. > Fig. 43

This also determines the sequence of the different trades:

1. Fitting the railing to the balcony slab
2. Installing the gutter in the intermediate space
3. Sealing the surface up to the gutter

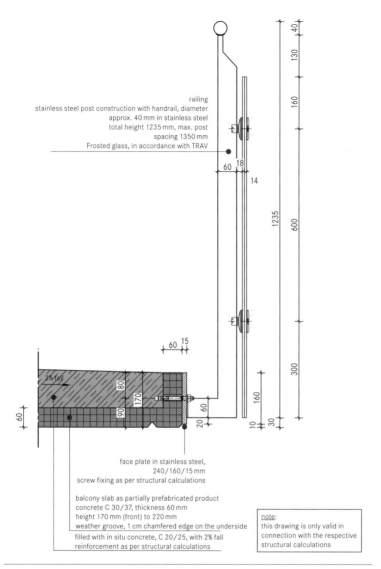

railing
stainless steel post construction with handrail, diameter
approx. 40 mm in stainless steel
total height 1235 mm, max. post
spacing 1350 mm
Frosted glass, in accordance with TRAV

face plate in stainless steel,
240/160/15 mm
screw fixing as per structural calculations

balcony slab as partially prefabricated product
concrete C 30/37, thickness 60 mm
height 170 mm (front) to 220 mm
weather groove, 1 cm chamfered edge on the underside
filled with in situ concrete, C 20/25, with 2% fall
reinforcement as per structural calculations

note:
this drawing is only valid in
connection with the respective
structural calculations

Fig. 42: Adding installation details of the railing

Now the parts of the floor structure and finish are added to the drawing. In this case, these consist of paving slabs, vertically adjustable bearing pads with protection membrane, and the bituminous sealing membrane already entered in the previous step. The user requested that the fall of the floor finish be less than that of the balcony slab (that is, 1.5%).

Completing the
section drawing

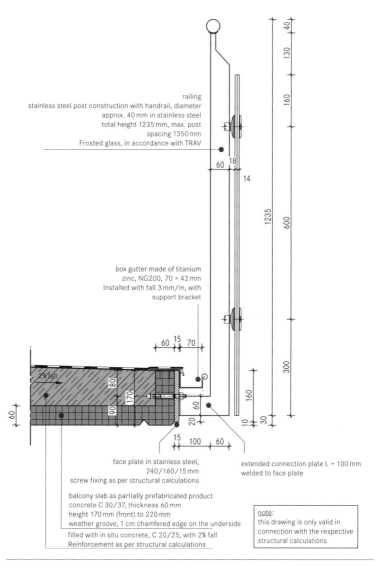

railing
stainless steel post construction with handrail, diameter
approx. 40 mm in stainless steel
total height 1235 mm, max. post
spacing 1350 mm
Frosted glass, in accordance with TRAV

box gutter made of titanium
zinc, NG200, 70 × 42 mm
Installed with fall 3 mm/m, with
support bracket

face plate in stainless steel,
240/160/15 mm
screw fixing as per structural calculations

balcony slab as partially prefabricated product
concrete C 30/37, thickness 60 mm
height 170 mm (front) to 220 mm
weather groove, 1 cm chamfered edge on the underside
filled with in situ concrete, C 20/25, with 2% fall
Reinforcement as per structural calculations

extended connection plate L = 100 mm
welded to face plate

note:
this drawing is only valid in
connection with the respective
structural calculations

Fig. 43: Entering the sealing membrane and gutter

In view of the fact that the floor construction is not the main concern of this detail, the respective annotation can be included in the general text block. Likewise, dimensions are only shown for the overall thickness of the floor structure. Given that the railing continues around the corner of the building, important view lines – such as the handrail and the contour of another post – are entered with a thinner, lighter line. > Fig. 44

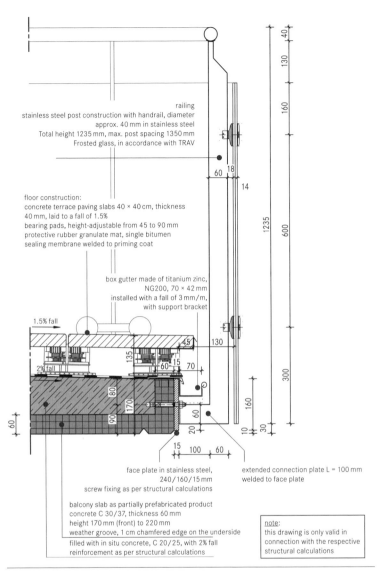

railing
stainless steel post construction with handrail, diameter
approx. 40 mm in stainless steel
Total height 1235 mm, max. post spacing 1350 mm
Frosted glass, in accordance with TRAV

floor construction:
concrete terrace paving slabs 40 × 40 cm, thickness
40 mm, laid to a fall of 1.5%
bearing pads, height-adjustable from 45 to 90 mm
protective rubber granulate mat, single bitumen
sealing membrane welded to priming coat

box gutter made of titanium zinc,
NG200, 70 × 42 mm
installed with a fall of 3 mm/m,
with support bracket

1.5% fall

2% fall

face plate in stainless steel,
240/160/15 mm
screw fixing as per structural calculations

extended connection plate L = 100 mm
welded to face plate

balcony slab as partially prefabricated product
concrete C 30/37, thickness 60 mm
height 170 mm (front) to 220 mm
weather groove, 1 cm chamfered edge on the underside
filled with in situ concrete, C 20/25, with 2% fall
reinforcement as per structural calculations

note:
this drawing is only valid in
connection with the respective
structural calculations

Fig. 44: Complete section drawing

At this stage it is advisable to check again the list of requirements, and compare it with the detail drawing.

First of all, it is important that all requirements are taken into account. In addition – and as evidence – each requirement should be represented in the drawing, including dimensions and, if applicable, an annotation. This means the appropriate dimensions and annotations

Checking fulfillment
of requirements

should be entered in the drawing. In this case, the annotations include a reference to the points at which ladders can be placed and where the gutter's drainage outlets are located. The minimum dimension of 90 cm from the top of the floor finish to the top of the handrail serves as a check that building control stipulations are complied with. The railing is also sufficiently high at the most unfavorable point, that is, at the highest point of the floor finish. In summary, the requirements of the previously compiled list have now been fulfilled.

It is often the case that, while creating the drawing, new requirements become apparent which previously were not, such as an improvement to the design.

In this example, a check has shown that the clear distance between the front edge of the balcony flooring and the glass pane of the railing is 13 cm, in spite of the overhang of the stone slab. This gap is too wide and represents a safety hazard.

To remedy the situation, round bars are added in the fields between the posts. > Fig. 45

The first detail drawing is now complete and the process has demonstrated how important it is to show complex details from several angles, and to check these details in all three dimensions.

In the next step, the existing section drawing is used to produce an external elevation. For the sake of greater clarity, some components of the drawing, such as text blocks and dimension chains, are temporarily hidden. Many details of the necessary edges of the objects to be shown are already given, and are extended like in a normal projection drawing. The dimensions of the objects in the view that hitherto was concealed are already known from the description, or have to be determined in the design. The elevation drawing of the railing is not shown in full but only in part, with the limiting lines shown as dash-and-dot lines. Concealed edges are shown as dotted lines, and the fixing axes are entered. > Fig. 46

In this case, the elevation drawing is shown with various infill areas in order to improve clarity. This helps to represent the overlay of the glass panels. The dimensions of important edges in the elevation drawing are shown, and any dimensions relating to new information are entered. Given that both drawings are shown close to and level with each other, existing dimension chains can be used for both parts. The objective of showing the dimensions is to cover every detail but avoid any duplication.

The same applies analogously to the annotations, which means that, in this example, no additional annotations are needed for the elevation drawing. Since the drawing now consists of more than one part, both the parts are given a title and the axis of the section drawing is shown in the elevation.

After adding another drawing from another angle, all three dimensions are included with the respective information. This makes it possible to check whether any parts collide at any point.

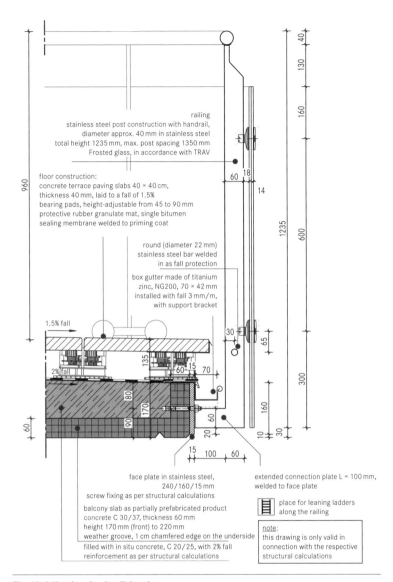

railing
stainless steel post construction with handrail,
diameter approx. 40 mm in stainless steel
total height 1235 mm, max. post spacing 1350 mm
Frosted glass, in accordance with TRAV

floor construction:
concrete terrace paving slabs 40 × 40 cm,
thickness 40 mm, laid to a fall of 1.5%
bearing pads, height-adjustable from 45 to 90 mm
protective rubber granulate mat, single bitumen
sealing membrane welded to priming coat

round (diameter 22 mm)
stainless steel bar welded
in as fall protection

box gutter made of titanium
zinc, NG200, 70 × 42 mm
installed with fall 3 mm/m,
with support bracket

1.5% fall

2% fall

face plate in stainless steel,
240/160/15 mm
screw fixing as per structural calculations

balcony slab as partially prefabricated product
concrete C 30/37, thickness 60 mm
height 170 mm (front) to 220 mm
weather groove, 1 cm chamfered edge on the underside
filled with in situ concrete, C 20/25, with 2% fall
reinforcement as per structural calculations

extended connection plate L = 100 mm,
welded to face plate

place for leaning ladders
along the railing

note:
this drawing is only valid in
connection with the respective
structural calculations

Fig. 45: Adjusting the detail drawing

In this example it is possible to ascertain that no collision exists between individual parts. The elevation drawing contains the additional information that the gutter holders are to be fitted outside the area of the face plates. > Fig. 47

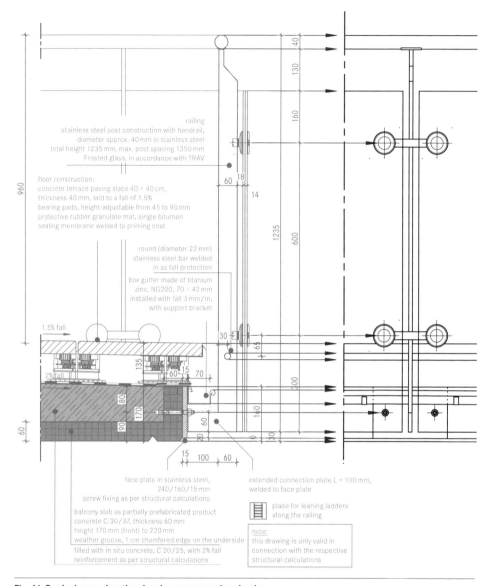

railing
stainless steel post construction with handrail,
diameter approx. 40 mm in stainless steel
total height 1235 mm, max. post spacing 1350 mm
Frosted glass, in accordance with TRAV

floor construction:
concrete terrace paving slabs 40 × 40 cm,
thickness 40 mm, laid to a fall of 1.5%
bearing pads, height-adjustable from 45 to 90 mm
protective rubber granulate mat, single bitumen
sealing membrane welded to priming coat

round (diameter 22 mm)
stainless steel bar welded
in as fall protection

box gutter made of titanium
zinc, NG200, 70 × 42 mm
installed with fall 3 mm/m,
with support bracket

1.5% fall

2% fall

face plate in stainless steel,
240/160/15 mm
screw fixing as per structural calculations

balcony slab as partially prefabricated product
concrete C 30/37, thickness 60 mm
height 170 mm (front) to 220 mm
weather groove, 1 cm chamfered edge on the underside
filled with in situ concrete, C 20/25, with 2% fall
reinforcement as per structural calculations

extended connection plate L = 100 mm,
welded to face plate

place for leaning ladders
along the railing

note:
this drawing is only valid in
connection with the respective
structural calculations

Fig. 46: Producing an elevation drawing as a second projection

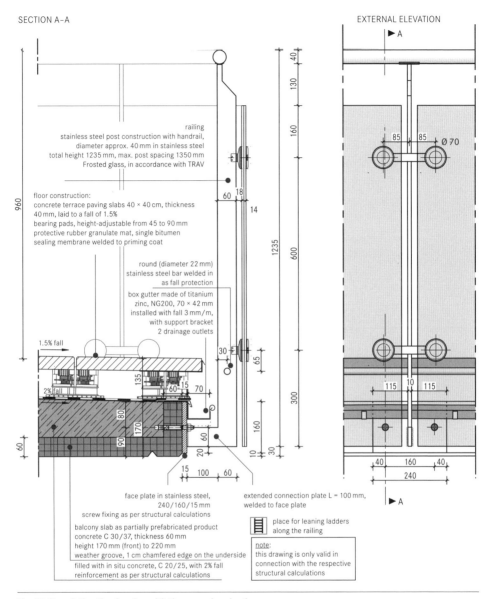

SECTION A–A

EXTERNAL ELEVATION

►A

railing
stainless steel post construction with handrail,
diameter approx. 40 mm in stainless steel
total height 1235 mm, max. post spacing 1350 mm
Frosted glass, in accordance with TRAV

floor construction:
concrete terrace paving slabs 40 × 40 cm, thickness
40 mm, laid to a fall of 1.5%
bearing pads, height-adjustable from 45 to 90 mm
protective rubber granulate mat, single bitumen
sealing membrane welded to priming coat

round (diameter 22 mm)
stainless steel bar welded in
as fall protection

box gutter made of titanium
zinc, NG200, 70 × 42 mm
installed with fall 3 mm/m,
with support bracket
2 drainage outlets

1.5% fall

2% fall

face plate in stainless steel,
240/160/15 mm
screw fixing as per structural calculations

balcony slab as partially prefabricated product
concrete C 30/37, thickness 60 mm
height 170 mm (front) to 220 mm
weather groove, 1 cm chamfered edge on the underside
filled with in situ concrete, C 20/25, with 2% fall
reinforcement as per structural calculations

extended connection plate L = 100 mm,
welded to face plate

►A

place for leaning ladders
along the railing

note:
this drawing is only valid in
connection with the respective
structural calculations

Fig. 47: Completing the drawing with the second projection

Objective-based Detail Design

In the previous chapter, we developed a detail drawing mainly from the point of view of construction. Starting from a basic idea as to how the different parts function together, a detail drawing is used to establish how this actually works out. The basic idea is often derived from experience or technical rules, such as those in DIN standards.

A different approach to developing a detail drawing is objective-based detail design. As a rule, this begins by formulating a certain objective, which may be of a conceptual nature, or it may be aimed at making a construction particularly effective. Other objectives can be those of
● optimizing quantities or reducing the required construction time.

As a rule, the formulated objective is approached step by step. As a starting point, a standard detail is used, in which the construction is shown in a straightforward manner, including all pertinent requirements. As the drawing is developed, the basic detail is modified at certain places in a stepwise process until the intended objective is achieved. It is important here to check that the detail still fulfills all known requirements after each modification.

Example: Edge of roof   In order to explain the approach used in stepwise optimization, we will use the example of a roof edge to try to optimize its construction with the objective of achieving as narrow and as uncluttered a visible edge as possible. The detail is that of the eaves of a projecting timber roof. Using the procedure explained in the previous chapters, we produce a detail drawing which is plausible from a functional point of view. In this case it is a rafter construction, with rafters extending beyond the eaves purlin and covered with roof sheathing at the top and with timber cladding at the bottom. For structural reasons, the vertical dimension of the rafters is 30 cm. Extensive planting has been planned for the surface of the roof, and the drainage is not to be run through the heated interior of the building. Consequently, a gutter has been provided at the end of the rafters that is connected to downpipes at two places along
○ the eaves. > Fig. 48

● **Example:** A conceptual objective could be formulated as follows: "The visible edge of a roof perimeter should be as narrow as possible." An example of optimizing the quantity could be: "The floor structure should be as minimal as possible."

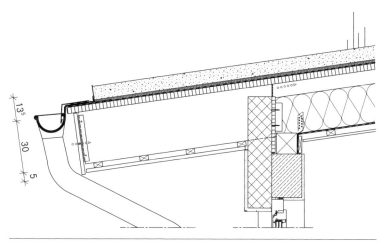

Fig. 48: Simple eave detail as a starting point

The vertical dimension of the rafters, the thickness of the underside cladding, and the thickness of the extensive planting with structure together add up to a total of 48.5 cm. In addition to this rather large eave dimension, the gutter attached to the rafter ends is considered to be detrimental, and it is thought that the swan necks of the downpipes do not result in an aesthetic appearance owing to the slope of the roof.

For this reason, the drainage element of this detail was revised.
> Fig. 49

In the first revision the roof drainage was changed from a linear gutter to a point drainage system. This means that the gutter and swan necks connecting with the downpipes can be omitted. The drainage point inlets were placed above the downpipes so that the routing of the downpipes is as straightforward as possible. This also has the advantage that the drainage point is further back from the eaves and is therefore not seen from the ground. This reduces the thickness of the roof structure above the rafters to 4.5 cm.

○ **Note:** For reasons of clarity the annotations have been omitted and the dimension lines have been reduced to a minimum in the following detail drawings.

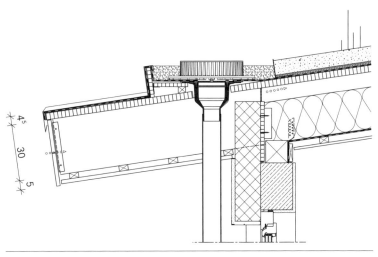

Fig. 49: First revision – concealed roof drainage

In the assessment it can be stated that this measure has achieved a clear improvement in terms of the visual appearance of the eaves detail. Nevertheless, in contrast with the formulated design intention, the detail of the rafter feet does not meet the objective of producing as slender a roof as possible. For this reason, the detail drawing was again revised. > Fig. 50

In the second step the geometry of the bottom end of the rafters was modified. In view of the fact that the structural load on the rafters is lower in the cantilevered part, the cross-section was reduced by 6 cm. Furthermore, the face was cut at an angle and the front edge was slightly recessed from the front edge of the roof sheathing. This means that the vertical front of the eaves only consists of the end flashing. The slightly recessed slanting fascia board is perceived to be separate from the vertical face.

These measures helped to achieve a significant improvement in the visual appearance of the eaves. The overall vertical dimension of the end flashing plus fascia has been reduced from 48.5 cm to 33.5 cm, and the two have been visually separated.

Regardless of the widespread use of digital media and mobile devices, the most common form of transmitting information between the designer and the contractors is still drawings on paper.

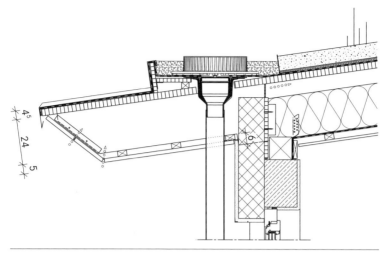

Fig. 50: Second revision – shaping the rafter feet

Choice of Medium

The advantages over digital media are more significant in the context of working on a construction site than in other spheres of work. Drawings in paper form are more resistant to the effects of wetness and dirt, as well as heat and cold, compared to digital media. In addition, it is easier to enter annotations and comments by hand and, on a large-scale drawing, it is possible to show – and see at a glance – a substantial amount of information and the points it relates to.

In order to benefit from digital information processing, it is advisable to establish a two-track system in which every printed drawing has a digital counterpart.

Drawing title block When producing drawings, it is particularly important to include a meaningful drawing title block. In general, drawing headers for technical drawings are designed in accordance with ISO 7200. > Fig. 51

However, in architecture it is common practice to adapt the content and arrangement of drawing title blocks to suit the complexity of the building project. Furthermore, it is quite common to use different drawing headers for the different design phases such as outline design, scheme design, presentation, approval, working drawings, and detail drawings. However, within a design phase the drawing title block should always be uniform. As a rule, templates for drawing headers are available in architectural practices or are specified by the client.

However, before distributing and filing drawings, the content of the drawing title block and the numbering of individual drawings should be checked for practicability and, if appropriate, should be revised.

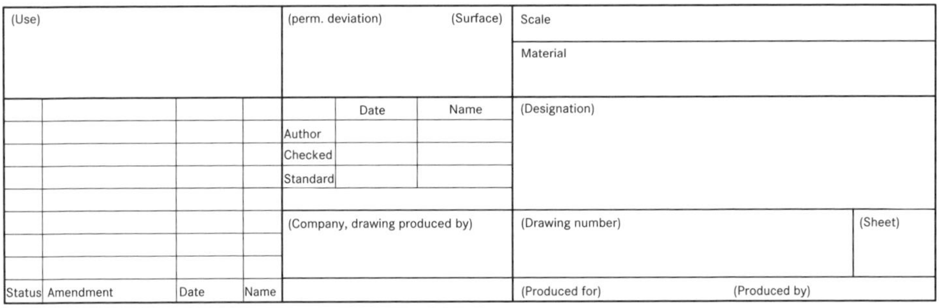

(Use)					(perm. deviation)		(Surface)	Scale		
								Material		
					Date	Name	(Designation)			
			Author							
			Checked							
			Standard							
			(Company, drawing produced by)			(Drawing number)			(Sheet)	
Status	Amendment	Date	Name			(Produced for)		(Produced by)		

Fig. 51: Drawing title block in accordance with ISO 7200

Minimum requirements for information in a drawing title block:

— Project name
— Address of construction site
— Client and client's address
— Author of the design and author's address
— Design phase
— Title/content of drawing
— Scale
— Direction north (in site plans and layout drawings)
— Reference point for level data
— Drawing number
— Creation date
— Author
— Drawing index with date
— List of amendments

The most important information should be shown on that part of the drawing that is uppermost and on the face of the drawing when it is folded. > Fig. 52

It may be useful to include the following additional information:

— Format of drawing
— Optical scale
— With large projects: block plan
— Sign-off by checker
— Sign-off for release

When printed plans are used in parallel with digital drawing information such as CAD data, it makes sense to use the same nomenclature for the digital file and the paper version, and to include an annotation in the drawing title block.

During the detail design phase, it is common for specialist engineers such as structural engineers, services engineers, and fire protection experts to be involved. In order to avoid lengthy inquiries, their respective contact data can be included in the drawing title block in a dedicated section.

The drawings produced in the detail design phase in particular contain many hatching symbols, abbreviations, and design symbols. Therefore all hatching and design symbols used should be listed and clearly explained in a legend. The same applies to the abbreviations used. Depending on the drawing format, such a legend can be placed in the upper part of the drawing title block, or near it. > Fig. 53

Legend

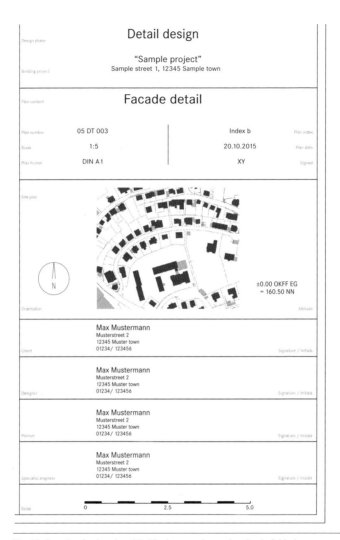

Detail design

Design phase

"Sample project"
Sample street 1, 12345 Sample town

Building project

Facade detail

Plan content

Plan number	05 DT 003	Index b	Plan index
Scale	1:5	20.10.2015	Plan date
Plan format	DIN A1	XY	Signed

Site plan

N

±0.00 OKFF EG
= 160.50 NN

Orientation

Altitude

Max Mustermann
Musterstreet 2
12345 Muster town
01234/ 123456

Client

Signature / Initials

Max Mustermann
Musterstreet 2
12345 Muster town
01234/ 123456

Designer

Signature / Initials

Max Mustermann
Musterstreet 2
12345 Muster town
01234/ 123456

Planner

Signature / Initials

Max Mustermann
Musterstreet 2
12345 Muster town
01234/ 123456

Specialist engineer

Signature / Initials

Scale

| 0 | 2.5 | 5.0 |

Fig. 52: Sample of a drawing title block seen when a drawing is folded

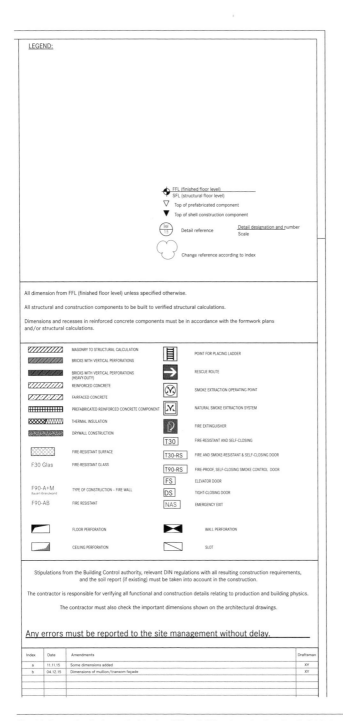

Fig. 53: Example of a legend; this should be visible when the drawing is folded

During the design phase it is quite common to place the title "Draft" on the drawing in a conspicuous fashion. This means that the drawing is not yet the final version for implementation in construction, and that modifications can be carried out at any time without any explicit reference annotations.

Once the design has been completed and approved by the client, the drawing is no longer a draft, it is the final version. The word *Draft* is removed from the drawing and the date of the drawing is entered in the drawing title block. In order to be able to track amendments to the final approved drawing, all amendment steps are listed in an index. Usually, letters in alphabetical order are used to identify the individual amendments. For the purpose of tracking changes it is advisable to enter such indices in the form of tables in the drawing title block, and to include a short description of each amendment.

For detail drawings in particular it is important to enter amendments carefully in the form of indices, because these drawings are directly used for the execution of construction work, usually very soon after their completion.

In drawings with a substantial amount of information, small amendments often cannot be spotted easily. For this reason, it is common to highlight any amendments contained in the respective amendment index with annotations in a bubble. > Figs. 54 and 55

Index	Date	Amendments	Draftsman
a	11.11.15	Some dimensions added	XY
b	04.12.15	Dimensions of mullion / transom construction	XY

Fig. 54: Amendment index

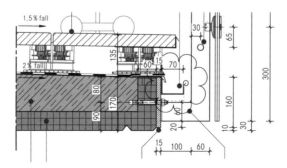

Fig. 55: Bubble to highlight amendment

In order to ensure that plans can be printed efficiently and without wasting paper, a number of different plan formats can be used, common ones being those of the DIN A series. Such plans can be reproduced relatively easily using large-format printers or plotters.

Plan format

Occasionally with detail drawings, the drawing title block takes up a large part of the plan, with its legend, explanation of abbreviations, and amendment index, while the actual drawing is rather smaller. In such a case, the sections of the drawing title block should be rearranged such that the plan is filled evenly.

In order to avoid confusion, placing several individual detail drawings on the same plan is something that should only be done in exceptional cases (for example, a detail collage in addition to the individual drawings). However, should it be necessary to place several individual drawings on one plan, it is important to ensure that it only includes drawings relating to the same detail, that is, eaves, ridge, or verges as the important details of a sloping roof. The name of the plan must be chosen to reflect its content, and the individual drawings must be clearly identified with their own titles. It is not advisable to include several individual drawings at different scales, since this can easily confuse those who have to work with the plan. The risk of confusion is particularly great when similar scales are used, such as 1:2, 1:2.5, and 1:5.

For larger projects it is advisable to compile all plans in a folder that contains all drawings relating to a particular design phase. For reasons of clarity, these plans should all be produced in the same format orientation (usually landscape).

For the purpose of sending or filing plans in folders, they are folded so that the final size is in A4 format; the method of folding is specified in DIN 824. If no folding machines are available, it is advisable to include fold marks on the plans at the appropriate locations.

Fold marks

Plans of any size should be folded such that the title block with the most important information is fully visible on the face of the folded plan, and it can be read without having to unfold the plan. This means that when a title block is chosen that deviates from the dimensions given in ISO 7200, it is important to ensure that the dimensions are nevertheless approximately DIN A4 size so that the entire block can be seen in a folded state.

Top face of folded plan

In the detail design phase in particular, it is possible for many plans to be produced depending on the size of the project. For effective management, it is usual to produce a separate index listing all existing plans with their respective numbers.

This list is made available to all those involved in the project, thereby reducing the risk of work being carried out using outdated plans. For documentation purposes and for tracking amendments, all outdated plans are archived separately from current ones. > Fig. 56

Document management

SECTION A-A

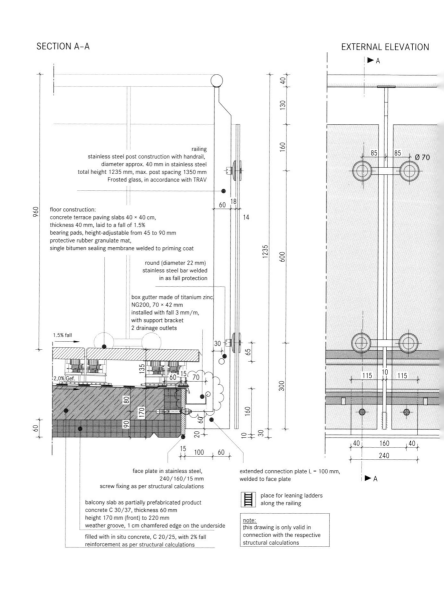

railing
stainless steel post construction with handrail,
diameter approx. 40 mm in stainless steel
total height 1235 mm, max. post spacing 1350 mm
Frosted glass, in accordance with TRAV

floor construction:
concrete terrace paving slabs 40 × 40 cm,
thickness 40 mm, laid to a fall of 1.5%
bearing pads, height-adjustable from 45 to 90 mm
protective rubber granulate mat,
single bitumen sealing membrane welded to priming coat

round (diameter 22 mm)
stainless steel bar welded
in as fall protection

box gutter made of titanium zinc,
NG200, 70 × 42 mm
installed with fall 3 mm/m,
with support bracket
2 drainage outlets

1.5% fall

2.0% Gef.

face plate in stainless steel,
240/160/15 mm
screw fixing as per structural calculations

balcony slab as partially prefabricated product
concrete C 30/37, thickness 60 mm
height 170 mm (front) to 220 mm
weather groove, 1 cm chamfered edge on the underside

filled with in situ concrete, C 20/25, with 2% fall
reinforcement as per structural calculations

EXTERNAL ELEVATION

►A

Ø 70

extended connection plate L = 100 mm,
welded to face plate

place for leaning ladders
along the railing

note:
this drawing is only valid in
connection with the respective
structural calculations

►A

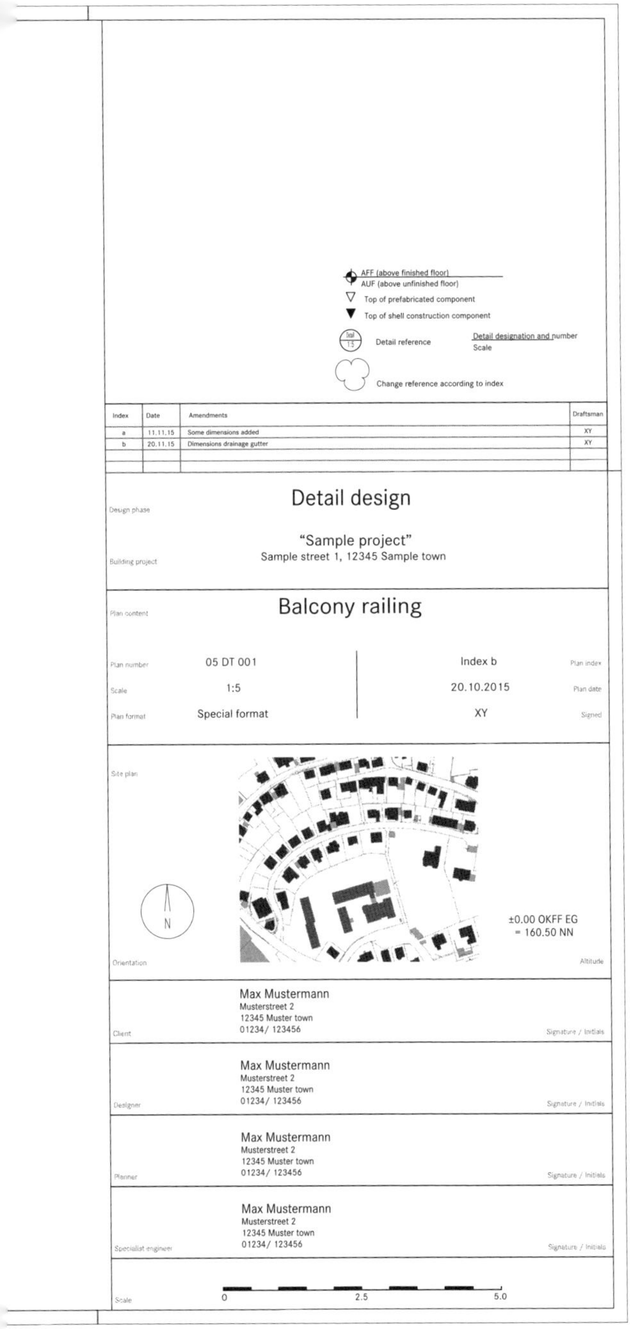

Fig. 56: Completed plan with detail drawings

Within the drawing/title block:

AFF (above finished floor)
AUF (above unfinished floor)
▽ Top of prefabricated component
▼ Top of shell construction component
Detail reference — Detail designation and number / Scale
Change reference according to index

Index	Date	Amendments	Draftsman
a	11.11.15	Some dimensions added	XY
b	20.11.15	Dimensions drainage gutter	XY

Design phase

Detail design

"Sample project"
Sample street 1, 12345 Sample town

Building project

Plan content

Balcony railing

Plan number	05 DT 001	Index b	Plan index
Scale	1:5	20.10.2015	Plan date
Plan format	Special format	XY	Signed

Site plan

±0.00 OKFF EG = 160.50 NN

Orientation — N

Altitude

Client
Max Mustermann
Musterstreet 2
12345 Muster town
01234/ 123456
Signature / Initials

Designer
Max Mustermann
Musterstreet 2
12345 Muster town
01234/ 123456
Signature / Initials

Planner
Max Mustermann
Musterstreet 2
12345 Muster town
01234/ 123456
Signature / Initials

Specialist engineer
Max Mustermann
Musterstreet 2
12345 Muster town
01234/ 123456
Signature / Initials

Scale
0   2.5   5.0

Appendix

ABBREVIATIONS

Abbreviations are frequently used in technical drawings in order to reduce the quantity of text without compromising the information content. In order to prevent drawings, in particular detail drawings, being overloaded with text, it is advisable to abbreviate generally known terms.

Tab. 2: Typical architectural abbreviations:

ACT	Acoustic Ceiling Tile		EJ	Expansion Joint
AD	Area Drain		EL	Elevation
AFF	Above Finished Floor		ELEC	Electrical
ALUM	Aluminum		EPDM	Ethylene Propylene Diene M-Class (Roofing)
ANOD	Anodized			
BSMT	Basement		EQ	Equal
BYND	Beyond		EXIST	Existing
BOT	Bottom		EXP JT	Expansion Joint
CIP	Cast In Place		EXT	Exterior
CHNL	Channel		FD	Floor Drain
CJ	Control Joint		FEC	Fire Extinguisher Cabinet
CLG	Ceiling		FIXT	Fixture
CLR	Clear		FLR	Floor
CMU	Concrete Masonry Unit		FO	Face Of
COL	Column		FND	Foundation
COMPR	Compressible		GA	Gauge
CONC	Concrete		GALV	Galvanized
CONT	Continuous		GWB	Gypsum Wall Board
CPT	Carpet		HC	Hollow Core
CT	Ceramic Tile		HM	Hollow Metal
CTYD	Courtyard		HP	High Point
DBL	Double		HR	Hour
DEMO	Demolish or Demolition		HVAC	Heating, Ventilating, and Air Conditioning
DIA	Diameter		IRGWB	Impact-Resistant Gypsum Wall Board
DIM	Dimension			
DIMS	Dimensions		ILO	In Lieu Of
DN	Down		INSUL	Insulation
DR	Door		INT	Interior
DWG	Drawing		MAX	Maximum
EA	Each		MO	Masonry Opening

MECH	Mechanical
MEMBR	Membrane
MIN	Minimum
MRGWB	Moisture-Resistant Gypsum Wall Board
MTL	Metal
NIC	Not In Contract
NO	Number
NOM	Nominal
OC	On Center
OH	Opposite Hand
OZ	Ounce
PCC	Pre-Cast Concrete
PLUMB	Plumbing
PLYD	Plywood
PNT	Paint or Painted
PT	Pressure Treated
PVC	Polyvinyl Chloride
RBR	Rubber
RCP	Reflected Ceiling Plan
RD	Roof Drain
REQD	Required
RM	Room
SIM	Similar
SPEC	Specification
SPK	Sprinkler
SSTL	Stainless Steel
STC	Sound Transmission Coefficient
STL	Steel
STRUCT	Structural
T&G	Tongue and Groove
TEL	Telephone
TLT	Toilet
TME	To Match Existing
TOC	Top of Concrete
TOS	Top of Steel
TPD	Toilet Paper Dispenser
T/D	Telephone/Data
TYP	Typical
UNO	Unless Noted Otherwise

U/S	Underside
VIF	Verify In Field
VP	Vision Panel
WD	Wood

STANDARDS

Many aspects of producing technical drawings are subject to uniform international standards. For that reason, important aspects are covered by ISO standards. In most countries the ISO standards are adopted by the national standards institutes. In Germany, these standards are referred to with "DIN ISO."

Tab. 3: Relevant ISO standards

ISO 128	Technical Drawings – General Principles of Presentation
ISO 3766	Construction Drawings – Simplified Representation of Concrete Reinforcement
ISO 4157	Construction Drawings – Designation Systems
ISO 5455	Technical Drawings – Scales
ISO 5456	Technical Drawings – Projection Methods
ISO 6284	Construction Drawings – Indication of Limit Deviations
ISO 7518	Technical Drawings – Construction Drawings – Simplified Representation of Demolition and Rebuilding
ISO 7519	Technical Drawings – Construction Drawings – General Principles of Presentation for General Arrangement and Assembly Drawings
ISO 8048	Technical Drawings – Construction Drawings – Representation of Elevations and Sections
ISO 8560	Technical Drawings – Construction Drawings – Representation of Modular Sizes, Lines, and Grids
ISO 9431	Construction Drawings – Spaces for Drawing and for Text, and Title Blocks on Drawing Sheets
ISO 10209	Technical Product Information
ISO 11091	Construction Drawings – Landscape Drawing Practice

In addition to the adopted ISO standards, national standards exist in Germany that have to be additionally taken into account.

Tab. 4: Relevant DIN standards

DIN 107	Building Construction – Identification of Right and Left Side
DIN 406	Dimensioning
DIN 824	Technical Drawings – Folding to Filing Size
DIN 919	Technical Drawings – Wood Processing
DIN 1080	Terms, Symbols, and Units Used in Structural Engineering
DIN 1356	Building and Civil Engineering Drawings
DIN 4172	Modular Coordination in Building Construction
DIN 6771-1	Title Blocks for Drawings, Plans, and Lists

LITERATURE

Batran, Balder, et al. *Construction Drawings – Architecture*, *Civil Engineering, Road Construction and Landscaping,* 5th ed. Hamburg: Handwerk und Technik, 2016

Bielefeld, Bert, and Isabella Skiba. *Basics – Technical Drawing,* rev. and exp. ed. Basel: Birkhäuser, 2011

Bielefeld, Bert, ed. *Basics – Architectural Drawing.* Basel: Birkhäuser, 2014

Bielefeld, Bert, ed. *Designing Architecture – Dimensions, Spaces, Typologies.* Basel: Birkhäuser, 2016

Deplazes, Andrea. *Architectural Construction – From the Raw Material to the Building: A Handbook,* 4th ed. Basel: Birkhäuser, 2013

Hoischen, Hans, and Andreas Fritz, eds. *Technical Drawing: Standards, Examples, Geometric Representation*, 35th ed. Berlin: Cornelsen, 2016

Moro, José Luis, and Matthias Rottner. *Building Construction – From the Principle to the Detail*, 2 vols. Wiesbaden: Springer, 2008

Simmons, Colin H., et al. *Manual of Engineering Drawing*, 4th ed. Oxford: Butterworth-Heinemann, 2012

Smith, Paul. *Drawing for Engineering*. Cape Town: Juta, 1999

PICTURE CREDITS

THE AUTHOR

Björn Vierhaus, Dipl.-Ing., architect from Siegen, assistant professor at the University of Siegen, Department of Construction Economics and Construction Management

Series editor: Bert Bielefeld
Concept: Bert Bielefeld, Annette Gref
Translation from German into English:
Hartwin Busch
English copy editing: Keonaona Peterson
Project management: Lisa Schulze
Layout, cover design and typography:
Andreas Hidber
Typesetting: Sven Schrape
Production: Heike Strempel, Amelie Solbrig

Library of Congress Cataloging-in-Publication
data
A CIP catalog record for this book has been
applied for at the Library of Congress.

Bibliographic information published by the
German National Library
The German National Library lists this publica-
tion in the Deutsche Nationalbibliografie;
detailed bibliographic data are available on the
Internet at http://dnb.dnb.de.

This publication is also available as an e-book
(ISBN PDF 978-3-0356-1392-6;
ISBN EPUB 978-3-0356-1397-1)
and in a German language edition
(ISBN 978-3-0356-1376-6).

© 2018 Birkhäuser Verlag GmbH, Basel
P.O. Box 44, 4009 Basel, Switzerland
Part of Walter de Gruyter GmbH, Berlin/Boston

Printed on acid-free paper produced from
chlorine-free pulp. TCF ∞

Printed in Germany

ISBN 978-3-0356-1379-7

9 8 7 6 5 4 3 2 1
www.birkhauser.com